READY OR NOT
THE LORD IS COMING!

JESUS LOVES YOU

WRITTEN BY
SUSAN FREE

Front/Back Cover: *Depiction of Rapture*: Designed and Illustrated by Chris Fechter.
Chapter illustrations designed by Chris Fechter
Editors: Debbie Bodenhamer, Chris Fechter, Michelle Nelson

COPYRIGHT @ by Susan Free 2015
Terrebonne, OR 97760
Printed by CreateSpace, an Amazon Company
Printed in the United States of America

ISBN: 978-0-9966069-0-5

Visit author's website:
 http://readyornotthelordiscoming.com

DEDICATION

To my grandchildren,
Jennifer, Max, Jaiden & Morgan
*"Jesus Loves You, Yes I Know,
For the Bible tells Me So."*

To my daughters, Julie & Michelle,
And step-daughters, Becky and Cindy,
May the Lord be in Your Lives, Forever!

Robert Free, life-time friend, husband, and partner;
You inspire me to be closer to the Lord!
Thank you for sharing your time,
So that I may follow the Lord!

ACKNOWLEDGMENTS

All the Glory goes to my personal savior, Jesus Christ. Without Him, I am nothing but a shell; with Him I aspire to be an eagle spreading my wings. This book is prayerfully His words, His thoughts, and His inspiration.

Special thanks to my dear friend, Chris Fechter, who with her graphic art talent designed the front and back cover and the chapter headings. At the same time, she wrote a children's book, *The Seed in the Master's Garden"* and we climbed through the rough terrain together of writing, designing, formatting, and publishing. My friend, Debbie Bodenhamer, completed the book by her "eye" for editing, spelling, "quotes within quotes" surrounded by periods, exclamation marks and question marks, which made me dizzy. My daughter Michelle organized the headers when I could no longer make heads or tails of them.

Thank you Donna Kelly, my special friend for life, for inspiring me to "keep" going even when I wasn't sure I could do it. Her faith encouraged me weekly.

Some people influence me without realizing that they make a difference: Bill & Debbie Page, home bible study on Revelation; Gemey Cameron (when is your book done?); and Roxanne Warf, Daisy Teske and Gail Harlow, who encouraged and believed in me. Thank you, Dr. David Jeremiah, Hal Lindsey and John Hagee for your weekly inspiration.

Thank you to my Christian friends and family at Ranch Chapel for all your love through the years. Jesus Christ, our savior, is indeed coming again to be our King of Kings, Lord of Lords!

INTRODUCTION

In my own Christian walk of twenty-five years, the words "The Lord is coming" have always seemed so far off in my mind, not even a "reality". I wasn't sure I even believed the words to be true. I assumed I would be dead before I had to worry about the Lord returning, so it was easy to remove from my mind. After all, if I was baptized, saved and believed in Jesus Christ as my one and only savior; I felt I was home free and didn't have to worry about anything else. I had my security blanket and life would go on as usual. Like many Christians, I have read the bible many times, but didn't always fully comprehend what was being stated when I read "the Lord is Coming", or "the End of the Age

Over the years, I have attended many bible studies both at church and different homes and Revelation has never been taught in my circle until recently. Perhaps as Christians, we weren't ready for it or avoided it because it seemed so far off from our life style here on earth. There are some pastors and ministers that have avoided teaching on Revelation because they were not sufficiently trained in seminary to speak on prophecy. One pastor I spoke with said "we should focus on loving and getting to know Jesus and not put fear in everyone". Although there is a lot of truth to this statement, once we walk through learning about Revelation, we have the golden opportunity and desire to get closer to God; therefore, eliminating our fears, and rejoicing in the coming of our Lord.

Revelation, the last book of the 66 books of the Bible, is one of the more difficult books to understand. From the seven churches, to the rapture, to the seven years of unrestrained evil called the tribulation, seven seals, seven bowls of God's wrath, the second coming of Christ, the 1000-

year Millennium Reign, Great White Throne Judgment, and finally to the New Heaven and New Earth. It can be overwhelming and confusing. I personally needed a "simple, concise and truthful" presentation of what all these terms mean and how do they flow on a linear time line. So, I set out on a personal journey with God to find a way to present these terms in a simple and concise manner that easily could be understand by everyone.

I started out by reading over 15 books on prophecy, reading the Holy Bible and watching TV pastors like David Jeremiah, Hal Lindsay, John Hagee, and Perry Stone, learning as much as I could absorb. At first, the volume of information was confusing and very overwhelming, but as I continued to read and learn, the information began to repeat itself and I began to grasp it and make sense out it.

My first thought was, wouldn't it be nice to have a simple, concise and truthful book that explained all of this in more simple terms? As I prayed about writing this book, God inspired me and led me to the right people who could help and guide me through this information. I am most grateful!

Most importantly, I had to ask myself "do I believe in my heart, my mind and my soul that the Lord is coming again to rule on earth?" If the rapture happened tomorrow, would I go up in the clouds to meet the Lord or would I be left behind? I felt like I needed to be sure that "I was living like I really belonged to the Lord".

Today, television, social media, and the news channels all keep us informed of the many changes in our world; changes that are happening very fast, and on a daily basis. Could God be revealing Himself in mysterious ways? We look at our homeland, America, and see not only the land of the free, but the land of the lost. Could the Lord be coming back, sooner than we think? Is America about to receive another economic shift during the upcoming end of the Shemitah cycle? Did you know that "the second coming of Christ" is mentioned 300 plus times in the New Testament? That is one out of every approximately 25 verses. It is crystal clear in the Word of the Bible that the Lord is coming and we all need to be ready! The question remains: Are we ready?

This book is a result of that journey explained in simple terms, which I hope answers many of the questions you may have about prophecy. The terms are arranged in a chronological order that may be helpful in your walk with the Lord. My hope is that Christians reading this will draw closer to the Lord for the time is near. My hope for non-believers is that they can open up their hearts and ask Jesus to reside within their heart and make Him their One and only savior. We are running out of time as the end times reveal sign after sign that we are getting closer to the day when the Lord will appear in the clouds to rapture up His Church. The answers are all God-breathed, complete with scripture, with references from many Bible scholars and their material.

"All Scripture is God-breathed and is useful for teaching, rebuking, correcting and training in righteousness, so that the man of God may be thoroughly equipped for every good work." **2 Timothy 3:16**

"But do not forget this one thing, dear friends: With the Lord a day is like a thousand years, and a thousand years are like a day. The Lord is not slow in keeping his promise, as some understand slowness. He is patient with you, not wanting anyone to perish, but everyone to come to repentance." **2 Peters 3:8-9**

TABLE OF CONTENTS

Introduction   5

Chapter 1   Am I Ready?   11

Chapter 2   Signs of the End of the Age   21

Chapter 3   Four Blood Moons   45

Chapter 4   America: Land of the Free & the Lost   55

Chapter 5   Warning America: The Shemitah   69

Chapter 6   Discovering Prophecies   79

Chapter 7   America in Prophecy   91

Chapter 8   The "Rapture"   99

Chapter 9   The "Tribulation"   115

Chapter 10   Second Coming of the Lord   131

Chapter 11   New Heaven & Earth   141

Chapter 12   Are you Ready?   147

Chapter 13   Live like you "Belong" to God   161

Chapter 14   Hallelujah, the Lord is Coming!   173

Notes & References   177
Ten Commandments   181
The Lord's Prayer   182

CHAPTER 1

AM I READY?

"Behold, I am coming soon!
Blessed is He who keeps the words
of the prophecy in this book."
Revelation 22:7

As I sat at my desk, preparing teaching notes for a women's bible study on prophecy, I came upon this scripture in the book of **Revelation 22:7**: The words **"Behold, I am coming soon! Blessed is He who keeps the words of the prophecy in this book."** Dumfounded, I sat back in my chair and asked myself these two questions: "Do I really believe in my heart that the Lord is coming back? Do I believe He is coming back **soon**?"

As I watch the evening news, I hear about the Supreme Court voting and approving same-sex marriage for lesbians and homosexuals; a large commercial Malaysian airliner disappears over the Indian Ocean, with 239 people aboard, never to be seen again; a co-pilot in France takes matters into his own hands and intentionally crashes a plane into the French Alps killing all 150 people aboard; nine people are killed while attending a bible study in South Carolina; twenty-one Christians are lined up on the beach and beheaded by ISIS; Syria's civil war kills 220,000 people; and yet another gruesome headline, "Jordanian pilot burned alive in cage", on the street, for everyone to watch. These are just a few of the barbaric headlines; yet there are many more brutal and overlooked headlines that fill our world with confusion and terror!

The Middle East is plagued with violence, rapes, and unrest as ISIS spreads terror throughout Iraq, Syria, Yemen, Turkey, Libya, Nigeria, France, Tunisian, Kenya and other countries. As ISIS takes over villages and cities, they behead men, women and children who are Christians and Jews, and refuse to convert to Islam. Did you know 60 countries around the world are fighting against ISIS?

Israel, God's promise land for the Jews, is on constant alert defending attacks from the Gaza Strip as Palestinians fire missiles set on destroying Israel. Russia has invaded Ukraine taking over Crimea and as of February 2015, 20,000 have been killed or wounded with approximately 1 million people misplaced from their homeland.

We look at our own land of America and watch the decline of moral values and standards as everyone fights for their "rights". America seems to be the land of **"rights"** rather than moral values.

The **"right"** to abort 56 million babies since the 1973 Wade vs Roe decision; abortions have become a method of birth control. Yes, there are situations when it is warranted, but most pregnancies aborted are deemed inconvenient to the woman and her lifestyle. (Exodus 20:13)

The **"right"** to be a lesbian or homosexual and marry the same sex in a union called traditional "marriage" (Supreme Court 2015 decision) and the **"right"** to force everyone else to accept it. (Roman 1:26-32) (Genesis: 1:27-28).

The **"right"** to commit a crime, disrespect police officers; resist arrest, and threaten a police officer, all without taking responsibility for the criminal action itself. The disrespect for law enforcement and general lawlessness is growly rapidly in our nation. (Exodus 20:15)

In God's eyes, all these **"rights" are "wrongs"**! We the people may vote for these "rights", but they are morally wrong, but God does ask us not to judge. He will do the avenging. Yet people, without knowing God, continue their daily ritual to prove that they are **"right"** demanding that people accept their **"right"** to kill, marry the same sex and steal when God does not condone these actions for our life.

Our own government has lost its way putting the nation eighteen (18) trillion in debt. If our home budgets experienced this type of debt, we would be bankrupt! Our government continues to weaken our military defense; refusing to unconditionally support our key ally Israel, and now negotiating a nuclear arms agreement with Iran, which is a nation set out to destroy Israel, and possibly the United States.

America, who once served as "One Nation under God", is now void of public reference to God, the Ten Commandments, and prayer in schools. For many Americans, Christmas is now Happy Holidays with little mention of Jesus; Easter is colored eggs and marshmallow peeps with little mention of Jesus dying on the cross and His resurrection; and Halloween, with its skeletons, crossbones and darkness, has become more popular than Christmas.

Most classrooms in schools across the nation cannot repeat the Pledge of Allegiance. In military organizations, the word "Jesus" cannot be used by military chaplains. What is happening to America? During the last 50 years, could the determination of America to disconnect God from our lives be at the final breaking point?

People are talking about the extreme weather events happening throughout the United States? Is God giving us warnings to turn to Him before He comes to judge the world? We are having extreme storms such as Hurricane Katrina, Hurricane Sandy, record snowfalls in Boston and the East Coast, plus one of the longest droughts in history in California. On my personal computer, I have an earthquake alert application and I can count, on any given day, hundreds of small to large earthquakes going on all over the world. The frequency of 4.0 plus earthquakes has increased in the past two months. The Pacific Ocean has an underwater, active volcano 300 miles off the Oregon coast, which is very unusual.

In Idaho, in March 2015, over 2000 geese mysteriously fell out of the air and died. Wildlife officials say they likely died from a disease causing the birds to die in midflight and drop out of the sky. In 2014-15, there have been several incidents of thousands of fish washing up on shore in Santa Cruz, California; Oahu, Hawaii, three miles of the Jersey shore, North Carolina, Lake Erie, Virginia and much to scientist's surprise, billions of jelly-like fish creatures have washed up on the West coast shores from Southern California to British Columbia. Search "google" and you will be surprised how many incidents come up.

I have only touched on just a "few" of the incidents going on around the world today. Most of them we never hear about on the news. Where is all this headed? Is it possible that God is giving us warnings of His upcoming judgment and signs as prophesized in the Bible that we are living in the "age of the end times"? Do we have our heads stuck in the sand not wanting to acknowledge how our world is changing?

In my own Christian walk of twenty-five years, the words, "The Lord is coming", has always seemed so far off in my mind, not even a reality. I assumed I would have died before I had to even worry about the Lord returning. After all, if I was baptized, saved and believed in Jesus Christ as my one and only savior; I felt I was home free and did not have to worry. I had repented of all my sins and sincerely wanted to change my life. I felt I had His stamp of approval and I was going to heaven. Yet, when I learned that God wants us to be 'real' Christians; *belong* to Him and *follow* Him, my whole attitude changed. I needed to do more research to fully understand "the End of the

Age" and to comprehend the full meaning of, "The Lord is coming".

After studying the Bible, prophecy and books from biblical scholars, the results have been staggering and eye-opening. It is not any one event that makes it seem like end times; it is the mass of prophecy coming together at one time that has my eyes wide open. My hope is that everyone can know the truth before it is too late. No, I am not famous or well-known like Billy Graham, John Hagee, or David Jeremiah, but I am a woman, mother, grandmother, sister, daughter, teacher, and a Christian with an extremely passionate heart to warn others that the "End of the Age", as we know it, is upon us. The end of the age is *not* the end of the world; it is the world changing and affecting how we live today.

"Blessed is He who reads and those who hear the words of this prophecy, and keep those things which are written in it; for the time IS near
(Revelation 1:3)

Billy Graham, well-known evangelical minister, stated in an exclusive interview with *Troy Anderson, president and editor-in-chief of the World Prophecy Network* that signs of the end of the age are "converging now for the first time since Jesus made those predictions." In his new book, *"The Reason for My Hope: Salvation,"* Graham wrote that the coming of Jesus Christ is near and the United States "can't go on much longer in the sea of immorality, without judgment coming." "We have been going down the wrong road for a long time," Graham said. "Seemingly, man has learned to live *without* God, preoccupied and indifferent

16

toward Him and concerned only about material security and pleasure.

He goes on to say, "The narrow road means that you forsake sin and you obey God, that you live up to the Ten Commandments and that you live up to the Sermon on the Mount desiring to please God in everything. The narrow road is hard and it is difficult; you can't do that yourself. You need God's help and that's the reason we ask people to come to receive Christ because when you receive Him, the Holy Spirit comes to live within to help us live the life."

Today, is it possible that God is revealing clues and giving us warnings about the end of the age? Could the Lord be coming back, sooner than we think? We will take a closer look at some of these mysterious happenings and you can decide for yourself. The "second coming of Christ" is mentioned 318 times in the New Testament; one out of every 25 verses. It is clear in the Word of the Bible that the Lord is coming and those who believe in Him will meet the Lord in the clouds when the rapture occurs.

Jesus told his disciples, "But of that day and hour no one knows, not even the angels in heaven, nor the Son, but only the Father. Take heed, watch and pray; for you do not know when the time is. And what I say to you, I say to all: "Watch"!   **(Mark 13:32-34, 37)**

Jesus states this several times in the Bible that no one knows the day or the hour, only the Father knows. He asks us to 'watch and pray' and repeats it profoundly by saying **WATCH**!   If we are left behind after the rapture, what will the world look like with millions of people disappearing? Following the rapture, people will experience the seven years of tribulation, which according to the Book of Revelation reveals life to be unbearable and full of suffering and hardship, nothing like we have seen before. How do we avoid the tribulation period?

There are so many questions and through prayer, the study of scripture in the Bible, and other prophecy books, God has inspired me to write this simple book to warn people that He is indeed returning to rule the earth. I believe there are many Christians today feeling confused with all the terminology of different prophecies, end times, rapture, tribulation, antichrist, second coming of Christ, 1000 years of millennium and new heaven and earth. My hope is to clarify these terms in a simple, easy manner.

One evening, after teaching my third class on prophecy, I remember sitting quietly in my living room when I saw a vision of Jesus from His head down to His waist. He

was framed in a small window that looks out over my yard. I was shocked to see that He had visibly, large tears running down His cheek and I heard His words, "Thank you, so few people believe I am really coming back." As I bowed my head in disbelief, my own tears fell as His words pierced my heart and it was then I felt the calling to write a simple book describing Jesus's return. How difficult it must be for the King of Kings and the Lord of Lords to love each of us the way He does and have billions of people refuse to acknowledge and come to know Him. In His loving heart, He does not want anyone to perish, but wants everyone to repent and trust in Him.

"But do not forget this one thing, dear friends: With the Lord a day is like a thousand years, and a thousand years are like a day. The Lord is not slow in keeping his promise, as some understand slowness. He is patient with

you, not wanting anyone to perish, but everyone to come to repentance." **(2 Peters 3:8-9)**

"All Scripture is God-breathed and is useful for teaching, rebuking, correcting and training in righteousness, so that the man of God may be thoroughly equipped for every good work." **(2 Timothy 3:16)**

As we look at our world, there are many questions to be answered. The nightly news offers us little light; only the evil and darkness of the world. Learn how to change your course by receiving Christ in your heart and living like you "belong" to God. The true and tried answers can be found only in the Bible. My hope is that you will continue to explore with me the answers God gives us for living with Him for eternity.

Before you decide to put this book down, please stay tuned for the shocking information about the warning signs God is mysteriously showing the world. We will explore together through scripture, prophecy, signs of the heavens and history, how God is preparing us for His return. We all need to be ready for the time is near! **Ready or Not: The Lord is coming!**

> **But of that day and hour no one knows, not even the angels in heaven, nor the Son, but only the Father. Take heed, watch and pray; for you do not know when the time is. And what I say to you; I say to all: Watch!**
>
> **(Mark 13:32-34; 37)**

READY OR NOT THE LORD IS COMING

CHAPTER 2

SIGNS OF THE END OF THE AGE

Does God have a plan for earth and the human race? If so, can man know it? The answer is yes, God does have a plan and that plan is clearly outlined in the Bible from the first book of Genesis to the last book of Revelation. Yes, reading the whole Bible from cover to cover may seem like an enormous task right now, but I hope you will put it on your 'bucket' list soon, for it holds all the answers for our present lives and our future.

Many believers want to understand the signs of the times and do so by researching scripture and learning about the rapture of the church, the tribulation and the eventual return of Christ. Other believers just want to know 'when' He will return and skip all the dialogue and study. Christians are naturally curious and discussing the visible signs that correlate with biblical prophecy satisfies their natural desire to try and figure out 'when' the rapture and second coming of Christ will happen.

The question of *'when'* was also asked by the Lord's disciples in **Matthew 24:3**: *"Tell us, when will these things be? And 'what' will be the sign of your coming, and of the end of the age?"* Jesus replied by telling the disciples the 'signs' of 'what' would be happening in the world. Jesus goes on to say in **Matthew 24:6-8**, *"And you will hear of wars* and rumors of wars. *See that you are not troubled; for all these things must come to pass, but the end is not yet. For nation will rise against nation, and kingdom against kingdom. And there will be famines, pestilences, and earthquakes in various places. All these are the beginning of sorrows."*

Now, we have all seen war and heard of nations fighting other nations; cultures or kingdoms fighting each other and we are all aware of famines, diseases and many earthquakes throughout our years here on earth. Jesus says that these are the beginning of sorrows. It is the accumulation of all these signs coming together at once with increased frequency and additional world chaos that causes Christians to be more WATCHFUL!

Now the word "sorrows" in the Hebrew language means "birth pangs", the pain in childbirth, which speaks of frequency and intensity. As a woman gets closer to giving birth, the "pangs" become more frequent and intense. This is also true for the signs of the end times. Throughout history we have seen the "pangs" (signs) become more frequent and intense, and in today's world the "pangs" are so frequent and intense that we must be ready for the delivery or the rapture, which happens when Jesus returns for His Church or His Bride. (His church or bride are His loyal followers.)

These prophetic signs would be indicators of events to pass before Christ's return. We need to be ready at all times for we do not know the hour or the day. The Lord will come like a thief in the night, a twinkling of an eye, and surprise us all. **(1 Thessalonians 5:1-2; 1 Corinthians 15:52).**

God's timing is not our timing on our wristwatch, calendars, or satellites. God's original time clock is in the lights of the sun, moon and stars. God has full control and only He can discern the times. As events collide, time will become squeezed or shortened and life will become more chaotic. We will then know that we have entered the period of the end of the age as we know it.

"And unless those days were shortened, no flesh would be saved; but for the elect's sake those days will be shortened.   **(Matthew 24:22)**

How do we know the signs we see are from God? The very first verse in **Genesis 1:1** states, *"In the Beginning, God created the heavens and the earth."* The heavens include the sun, moon, stars and the entire universe. This sentence is simple and profound. GOD created the heavens and the earth. God was already there before time began while the earth was without form and void; and dark. If a person believes Genesis 1:1 to be true then the rest of the Bible is considered to be true. It does not say MAN created the earth, nor does it say man evolved from primates, but that Man was created by God "in the image of God". God is "Almighty God", the Alpha and the Omega, the Beginning and the End.

GOD is present over all "creation" and guides, loves, and disciplines. Simply said, everything and anyone created on earth belongs to God. **Psalms 19:1** says, *"The heavens declare the glory of God and the firmament (space) shows His handiwork."* This Psalm points out that God has chosen to reveal Himself in two areas: the heavens referring to the sky above including the sun, moon and stars; and the "firmament", the expanse of God's creation. God is supreme over the sun, moon, stars and the entire universe and in **Genesis 1:14:** "Then God said, *"Let there be lights in the firmament of the heavens to divide the day from the night; and let them be for <u>signs and seasons,</u> and for days and years; and let them be for lights in the firmament of the heavens to give light on the earth"*; and it was so.

Genesis 1:16: *"Then God made two great lights; the greater light to rule the day and the lesser light to rule the night. He made the stars also."* God made the "sun" to rule the day and the "moon" and "stars" to rule the night. The Bible declares from the very beginning of time that God created the sun, moon and stars to divide day from night, but He also made them to be used for **signs** and **seasons**, and for days and years. According to the Strong Expanded Dictionary, The Greek word *seme*ion denotes a **"sign"** as a signal, mark or warning. The word **"seasons"** apply to not only our four seasons of spring, summer, fall and winter of the year, but the seasons or **"times"** of our life.

"But concerning the times and the seasons, brethren, you have no need that I should write to you. For you yourselves know perfectly the day of the Lord so comes as a thief in the night. For when they say, "Peace and safety!" then sudden destruction comes upon them, as labor pains upon a pregnant woman." **(1 Thessalonians 5:1-3)**

Let's take a closer look at our world today and identify ten (10) prophetic signs that are unfolding indicating we are in the End of the Age as we know it. This does not mean the world is ending; it means God is giving us prophetic "signs and signals"; that we are in the end of the age or end times. Signs include the fulfillment of prophecy, which is history written in advance. In the Old Testament, God determined

24

hundreds of years ago what would happen in history and then He carried it out. Our generation is blessed to actually *watch* some of these prophecies being fulfilled in our time.

1) Rebirth of Israel in 1948; official treaty signed May 14, 1948.

Bible passage: Amos 9:11, 13
Written: About 750 BC

Amos 9:11 *"On that day I will raise up the tabernacle of David, which has fallen down, and repair its damages; I will raise up its ruins, and rebuild it as in the days of old."* King David ruled Israel from about 1010 BC to about 970 BC and this land was conquered, destroyed and laid in ruins for much of the past 2000 years. The most pivotal day in Human History was on that day of May 14, 1948 when the United Nations announced "the natural right of the Jewish people is to be masters of their own fate, like all other nations, we therefore declare the establishment of the Jewish State to be known as the State of Israel". **Isaiah's prophecy in 66:8,** written 740 years before the birth of Jesus declared: ***"Who has heard such a thing? Who has seen such things? Shall the earth be made to give birth in one day? Or shall a nation be born at once?"*** In Isaiah, the prophet foretold the rebirth of Israel. He speaks of a country being born in one day. This is precisely what happened on May 14, 1948; Israel was declared a nation for the first time in 2000 years. The official United Nations treaty was signed in 1949. Prophecy fulfilled.

2) The Jews, scattered throughout the world, return to Israel.

Bible Passage: Ezekiel 36:24

Written: Between 593-571 BC

Ezekiel 36:24:   *"For I will take you from among the nations, gather you out of all countries, and bring you into your own land."*   The Jews, who were scattered all over the world, have been returning to their ancient homeland since the late 1800s. But, when Israel was declared a nation in 1948, millions of Jews began returning to their homeland. Today, it is estimated that 6.2 million Jewish people reside in Israel. In **Ezekiel 36:24-28**, the Lord says that He will take the Jewish people out of among the nations, gather them from all the lands and bring them into their own land, Israel. He will give them a new heart and put a new spirit in them. The Jews will be the people belonging to God and He will be their God. This prophecy has continued to be fulfilled since 1948.

3) Israel will prevail over its enemies; six day war in 1967.

Bible Passage: Isaiah 41:10, 12-13
Written: Between 701-681 BC

Isaiah 41:10, 12-13 Israel is assured of God's help, *"Fear not, for I am with you; Be not dismayed, for I am your God. I will strengthen you, Yes, I will help you; I will uphold you with My righteous right hand."* *"Those who war against you shall be as nothing, as a nonexistent thing. For I, the Lord your God, will hold your right hand, saying to you, 'Fear not, I will help you'."*

In June of 1967, the world witnessed the armies of Egypt, Jordan, Syria, Lebanon, Iraq, Algeria, Kuwait, Sudan and the whole Arab nation poised on the borders of little, but mighty Israel, ready to "wipe Israel off of the map." Their main objective was the destruction of Israel. The world was stunned when Israel nearly destroyed the entire Egyptian and Jordanian air forces as well as half of Syrian's armed forces and that was just on the first day. By the end of the six day war, Israel had recaptured Jerusalem, the Sinai, Golan Heights, Gaza Strip and West Bank and conquered enough territory to triple the size of Israel from 8,000 to 26,000 square miles." God is presenting a clear message from years ago, **"Those who war against you shall be as nothing".** A new bumper sticker might read: Don't Mess with Israel, My Promised Land! Since 1967, many nations have attacked Israel with the intentions of destroying her, but God is true to His word—Israel stands! Today, Iranian protesters have stated the very words, "wipe Israel off of the map" and "destroy America". This is something we need to WATCH! Prophecy fulfilled.

4) Trees would grow in Israel; Fruits would fill the world.

Bible Passages: Isaiah 41:19-20; Amos 9:13, Isaiah 27:6

Written: Between 701-681 BC

Isaiah 41:19-20 "I will plant in the wilderness the cedar and the acacia tree, the myrtle and the oil tree; I will set in the desert the cypress tree and the pine and the box tree together. That they may see and know, and consider and understand together, that the hand of the Lord has done this, and the Holy One of Israel has created it."

Can you imagine Isaiah, the prophet, writing 600-700 years before Christ was born, what currently coincides with modern day Israel? For 2000 years this land was desolate, barren of water and when the Jews returned during the

1900's, they built irrigation systems and more than 200 million trees have been planted in Israel.

Amos 9:13-15 *"Behold the days are coming," says the Lord, "When the plowman shall overtake the reaper, and the treader of grapes him who sows seed."* They have been rebuilding Israel's ancient cities, planting and harvesting the barren land. They use some of the most advanced farming and irrigation techniques to grow their crops. Today, Israel is a landscape of beautiful green hillsides, flowers, and bountiful crops such as grapes, fruit trees, and vegetables. God has done what He promised; brought back the Jews to Israel; rebuilt the cities and planted the land in vineyards, gardens, and fruit. They furnish food for many different countries.

Isaiah 27:6 *"Israel shall blossom and bud, and fill the face of the world with fruit."* Today the land of Israel is a leading producer of agricultural products exporting food to many other countries.

5) Technology Explosion
Bible Passage: Daniel 12:4
Written: 450-500 BC
Daniel 12:4 *"But you Daniel, shut up the words, and seal the book until the time of the end; many shall run to and fro, and knowledge shall increase."* Many running to and fro may indicate a search for answers; perhaps spiritual answers. Yet how many times today do you hear people talking about how fast-paced life is and how the days fly by so fast? We are a generation of people on the "move" in

airplanes, trains, and cars; eating "fast" food on the "run", and rarely sitting still until we fall into bed.

We have seen in our generation an "explosion of electronic technology" from radio, television, computers, cell phones, internet, tablets, watches, GPS, applications for almost everything under the sun, advanced computerized medical equipment, remote controls to fly an airplane or drone without a pilot, and the use of satellites to transmit signals across the globe in seconds. Cell phones, tablets, and software are changing at such warp speed that, for many of us, this explosion of technology is overwhelming as it quickly fluctuates year after year. We are definitely running to and fro with knowledge increasing. Prophesy Fulfilled.

6) Violence and Sexual Immorality

Bible Passage: Matthew 24:7; Luke 17-28-30
Written: Between 50–70 AD
Matthew 24:37-38 *"But as the days of Noah were, so shall also the coming of the Son of man be. For as in the days before the flood, they were eating and drinking, marrying and giving in marriage, until the day that Noah entered the ark…"*

Luke 17:28-30 *"Likewise also as it was in the days of Lot; they did eat, they drank, they bought, they sold, they planted, they built; But the same day that Lot went out of Sodom it rained fire and brimstone from heaven, and destroyed them all. Even thus shall it be in the day when the Son of man is revealed."*

What was it like in Noah's day and Lot's day? Violence prevailed during the days of Noah as **Genesis**

29

6:13 tells us. Sexual immorality, including homosexuality, prevailed during Lot's day. **Jude 1** says that Sodom and Gomorrah had given themselves over to "sexual immorality and gone after strange flesh".

As you look at our world today, violence is increasing at an alarming rate. All you have to do is turn on the television and you see ISIS and other groups fighting and killing with beheadings, burnings, rapes, and other barbaric acts. Here in America, lawlessness is beginning to take hold with less respect for police and other authority figures.

Sexual immorality has become the "norm" instead of God created man/woman relationships. We hear about more gang rapes on college campuses; more couples living together vs choosing marriage; births of babies without marriage; extra-marital affairs; homosexuality; pornography; children pornography; pedophiles, and abortions. Since 2001, many States have granted homosexuals the right to legally marry and on June 27, 2015, the Supreme Court of the United States voted and approved legalizing homosexual marriages in all 50 States. This would be another sign of the end times as Jesus predicted in Matthew 24:37-38. Prophecy fulfilled.

7) FAMINES AND PESTILENCES

Bible Passage: Matthew 24:7-8
Written: AD 50-60

Matthew 24:7-8 "For nation will rise against nation, and kingdom against kingdom. And there will be famines, pestilences, and earthquakes in various places. All these are the beginning of sorrows."

There have been hundreds of famines since 441 BC when the first recorded famine was located in Ancient Rome. According to Wikipedia, "Recent history shows that in 1996 North Korea estimated that 200,000 to 3.5 million people died of starvation. In the Democratic Republic of the Congo during the years 1998-2004, it is predicted that 3.8 million people died from starvation and disease."

In the last 30 years there have been millions of people around the World dying of starvation and disease resulting in an ongoing global food crisis. Many population groups do not have the financial means to even purchase food.

According to www.independent.co.uk, "For the first time in recent history, during the past 12 months, humanitarian organizations have had to respond to three serious food crises in West Africa, Yemen and East Africa. Almost a billion people are now hungry and the number of acutely malnourished children has risen for the first time this decade. More than 2.5 million children die from malnutrition each year."

On June 22, 2015, World Vision reports, "In Somalia, lack of rain and ongoing conflict has left nearly 3 million people in desperate need; just as this long-suffering country had begun to recover from a famine that killed a quarter of a million people". Suffering people tell World Vision staff, "This is the worst drought we have ever seen."

Pestilence means a deadly and overwhelming disease that affects an entire community. The Black Plague disease killed over 60% of Europe's population during 1346-53, numbering 50 million people. This Black Plague is "the greatest catastrophe every recorded."

During the 20th century alone, it is estimated that "smallpox" killed between 300-500 million people. The Great Chinese Famine of 1958-1961 killed between 15 and 43 million people over the span of three years. One of the most deadly diseases is malaria. The mosquito itself is the carrier, but certainly a death path for the over one million people each year who contact one of the 15 diseases manifested by a mere mosquito. Mosquitoes are capable of spreading many blood-borne illnesses containing parasites. Malaria is among the leading causes of premature death in the world, second only to HIV/AIDS in Africa.

At the end of 2013, HIV/AIDS, around the World, has been one of the largest epidemics of disease. Since the beginning of HIV, almost 78 million people have been infected and it is estimated 39 million people have died from HIV. Sub-Saharan Africa remains most severely affected with nearly 1 in every 20 adults living with HIV.

Today we see diseases such as Ebola, Marburg, Enterovirus, Bird Flu and others. These diseases were not even on the radar of most people beginning in 2014, yet each of them is making headline news. So why is this happening? Why are so many deadly diseases breaking out all over the world right now? Fortunately, in America we haven't seen plagues killing large percentages of our population. We have seen AIDS, bird Flu, Enterovirus, and other diseases, but on a smaller scale due to our advanced medical technology. Other countries in the Middle East and Africa are not so fortunate. (Prophecy fulfilled)

8) Nations will Rise Against Nations

Bible Passage: Luke 21:10; Matthew 24:6-7
Written: AD 50-60

Luke 21:10 Then He said to them, "Nation will rise against nation and kingdom against kingdom."

Over the years and years of history there have been so many wars, so it may not seem like this is an end time sign. If you turn on the news today, you can't help but notice that more nations; especially in the Middle East, are fighting among each other. Nations like Syria, Iraq, Iran, Egypt, Libya, Afghanistan, Russia, and Turkey have been fighting for years. When you look at the frequency and intensity of these wars, you begin to see that it is a sign of the end times.

According to the International Relations website on armed conflicts in the world today, they reported 32 conflicts in 2014 with Syria being the bloodiest war by far." According to Wikipedia, "the Syrian unrest began with nationwide protests against President Bashar al-Assad's government, who then responded with violent crackdowns. This conflict grew to a rebellion resulting in months of turmoil and by July 2013, the government had lost control of 60-70% of their land and 40% of their Syrian population. The Islamic Front joined other rebels in Syria and by July 2014, ISIS controlled a third of Syria's territory and most of its oil and gas production. As of January 2015, the death toll has risen above 220,000. In addition, tens of thousands of people have been imprisoned for protesting and another 6.5 million Syrians have been displaced or have fled to other countries such as Turkey, Lebanon, Jordan, Iraq and Egypt. Millions of refugees are living in poor conditions with a shortage of food and drinking water".

Unfortunately, this scenario is happening over and over again in the Middle East and Africa with ISIS furthering their advance into many other nations such as Egypt, Iraq, Yemen, Turkey, Tunisian, Libya, Kenya, Nigeria, Lebanon and many more. Wikipedia states that over 60 countries are currently waging war against ISIS.

In **Matthew 24:33**, Jesus said..."*when you see all these things, know that it is near----at the doors!*" Is war an end-time sign? Taking one sign like this does not prove we are living in the end times, but when you see "all these things" working together, we can't help but get excited about prophecy and the coming of our Lord.

9) There will be Earthquakes in various places

Bible Passage: Luke 21:11; Matthew 24:7
Written: AD 50-60

Luke 21:11 "And there will be great earthquakes in various places."

According to Oregon Live website, during the period of June 1-3, 2015, "Nine earthquakes in less than 3 days shook the ocean floor 300 miles off the Oregon Coast." These clusters of quakes were centered near the meeting of the Juan de Fuca and Pacific plates. These earthquakes, along with an active volcano erupting under the Pacific Ocean in the same area, are examples of "swarms" of activity that ask us to be watchful, alert and on guard.

Since I am a Native Oregonian, this scripture came to light when the local news reported on May 1, 2015, a rare volcano is erupting on the Pacific ocean floor about 300 miles off the coast of Oregon. On my laptop earthquake alert app, I noticed seven more earthquakes of 4.0 or more were off of the Oregon coast on June 1, 2015.   I thought of the scripture **Matthew 24:7** and what a "various or diverse place" this is and it is right in my own backyard.

The website, Crystalinks, states, "No one should be surprised if a magnitude-9 mega quake erupts off America's West Coast - or anywhere else around the Pacific Ocean's "Ring of Fire," for that matter." That's the upshot of a study in October's issue of the Bulletin of the Seismological Society of America: Researchers say that computer models of future seismic activity, plus a check of past activity going back thousands of years, suggest most of the Pacific's earthquake zones are capable of generating shocks at least as strong as magnitude 9 every 10,000 years on average.

We have all heard about earthquakes for years and many people may scoff that earthquakes are a sign of end times.   Remember we are talking about the intensity and frequency of signs during the last days.   Take a look at the following information and judge for yourself.

A new study finds there were more than twice as many big earthquakes in the first quarter of 2014 as compared with the average since 1979.   Tom Parsons, a research geophysicist with the U.S. Geological Survey (USGS) in Menlo Park, California states, "We have recently experienced a period that has had one of the highest rates of great earthquakes ever recorded."

The worldwide trend of alarmingly increasing earthquake strength and frequency are showing up in current graphs in the USGS statistical pages.

The Guardian Liberty Voice website states: Las Vegas, Nevada – "At approximately 11:42 Pacific Standard Time,

May 22, 2015, Nevada was hit with a rather strong 5.4 earthquake. With the largest reported earthquake in Nevada history, 7.1 magnitudes, having occurred exactly one hundred years ago; it may be wise to be guarded, following a temblor of this size." During the last 30 days there have been a swarm of earthquakes occurring in the area between Las Vegas and Tonopah, NV. The timing of earthquakes in Nevada with the release of the new movie "San Andrea" on May 29, 2015 is remarkable. The movie speaks to the swarm of earthquakes in the Nevada/Hoover Dam area. California and Alaska have multiple earthquakes every day, most of them smaller in size. On May 22, 2015, my earthquake app counted 117 earthquakes in California during a 24 hour period.

We also hear reports of multiple earthquakes in Oklahoma, Yellowstone National Park, Kansas, Puerto Rico, Nepal, Solomon Islands, Japan, Alaska, California, and many others all over the World.

These are just a few examples of various places earthquakes are occurring. If you want a much broader picture of earthquake activity and frequency around the world, check out this website showing current activity: (**earthquake**.usgs.gov/**earthquakes**). As of February 2015, there were approximately 3,100 earthquakes happening each month. Again, one or two earthquakes by themselves are not justification for an end-times sign. It is the frequency and intensity all over the World that justifies an end-time sign. (Prophecy fulfilled)

Revelation 16:18-19 "And there was a great earthquake, such as was not since men were upon the earth, so mighty an earthquake and so great. And the *great city was divided into three parts, and the cities of the nations fell."*

10) Christians & Jews will be Killed

Bible Passage: Deuteronomy 28:65
Written: 1406 B.C.

Deuteronomy 28:65 *"And among those nations you shall find no rest, nor shall the sole of your foot have a resting place; but there the Lord will give you a trembling heart, failing eyes, and anguish of soul."*

Matthew 24:9-14 *"Then they will deliver you up to tribulation and kill you, and you will be hated by all nations for My name's sake. And then many will be offended, will betray one another, and will hate one another. Then many false prophets will rise up and deceive many. And because lawlessness will abound, the love of many will grow cold. But he who endures to the end shall be saved. And this gospel of the kingdom will be preached in all the world as a witness to all the nations, and then the end will come."* This scripture represents the time of the second coming of Christ.

The panorama of prophecy that relates to the Jews is breathtaking. It applies to the past, the present, and the future. It demonstrates God's love and grace as nothing else does except the Cross itself. Christians and Jews have been killed for their faith all during the first century, as well as during the dark ages when the Roman Catholics ruled the world and killed millions of God's people. Today, this is being repeated all over the Middle East, Africa and Asia in countries such as Syria, Iraq, Iran, China, North Korea, Pakistan, Libya, Nigeria, India, Egypt, and many more. Although Christians and Jews in America and Europe are exposed to verbal persecution, they are not, at this time in history, exposed to massive attacks on their lives or facilities.

WE ARE LIVING IN END TIMES

There are many gospels being preached out in the world. The true gospel of Jesus Christ is to be preached to the world before the end. Is this one of the end-time signs? I believe it is because God's people are preaching the gospel through internet, television, satellite, radio, missionary work, bibles and books, churches, friends and family. We have all the resources to reach millions of people every day throughout the world. We are living in a time like no other and the gospel message is soon to reach the final corners of the earth, and then the final stages of this earth's history will take place. Yes, this end-time sign is being fulfilled. Prophecy fulfilled.

I hope that it is apparent from the above Biblical signs of the end times, that our generation is truly living in the last days, nearing the rapture, seven year tribulation and second coming of Christ Jesus. We are living in a time like no other. The world is being turned upside down and we need to be ready! If you are not a Christian and are wondering what you need to do to be saved, please continue reading to the end of this book to learn how to give your heart to Christ Jesus. He is about to return to bring judgment upon the whole world.

"So likewise ye, when ye shall see all these things, know that it is near, even at the doors. Verily I say unto you, this generation shall not pass, till all these things are fulfilled." **(Matthew 24:33-34)**

God is giving us plenty of warning through these events, and we will be without excuse if that day of Christ's return comes upon us like a thief in the night and catches us unaware. We need to heed the signs and be ready!

The Lord Himself is asking us to be ready for He is coming at an hour we do not expect. What does it mean to "be ready"? If you knew a thief was going to break into your home, but you did not know the exact hour, wouldn't you still want to be prepared? Perhaps you would check the locks on your doors and windows, alert the police, alert your neighbors, take your family to a safer place so they wouldn't get hurt; arrange protection for yourself by arming yourself with a weapon and then stand guard all night and WATCH! That is exactly what the Lord is asking of us; to be prepared and WATCH for He will come quickly!

To prepare ourselves for the Lord, we need to bring Him into our hearts; to accept Jesus genuinely into our heart; repent or be sorry for our wrongs or sins; ask Him for forgiveness; and return to a faithful relationship with Him by following and being obedient to Him. The last three chapters of this book will offer guidelines on how to follow and be obedient to Jesus.

Just like our earthly father, our heavenly Father will give us life and love us if we are obedient and follow. He will guide us through life, but if we do not follow His commandments, we will be judged and disciplined. I can remember many times in my life when I did not follow God and His darkness surrounded me. He didn't answer my prayers in the way I thought He would; He didn't offer any light around me; just depressing darkness. At that moment,

I knew I was in the wrong place doing the wrong thing. When I realized what was happening, I took steps to change my circumstances and do the right thing in God's eyes. Is it possible that our Lord will return with His wrath to judge, discipline, and dispel all darkness? If you are not a believer of Jesus Christ when He comes, you will be considered part of that darkness!

In Revelation, in the last chapter of the New King James Version, (NKJV) there are two sections written as "A Warning" and "I Am Coming Quickly". **Revelation 22:18-20** states, *"For I testify to everyone who hears the words of the prophecy of this book: If anyone adds to these things, God will add to him the plagues that are written in this book; and if anyone takes away from the words of the book of this prophecy, God shall take away his part from the Book of Life, from the holy city, and from the things which are written in this book. He who testifies to these things says, 'Surely, I am coming quickly'. Amen. Even so, come, Lord Jesus!"*

The Bible plainly declares there will be signs in the heavens, especially concerning the end of time or the end of the age, as we know it. Revelation clearly states and "warns" us that there is a final invitation for Christ to come back to the world and for the world to come back to Christ.

In **Revelation 21:6**, Jesus spoke and said, *"It is done! I am the Alpha and the Omega, the Beginning and the End; I will give of the fountain of the water of life freely to him who thirsts. He who overcomes shall inherit all things, and I will be his God and he shall be My son"*. Jesus spoke and said that anyone who "thirsts" for Him and "overcomes" shall inherit all things and I will be His God. Did you notice that this is not a multiple choice statement? Jesus spoke, "It is done!" He is the Beginning and the End!

We have to start with Genesis before we read the prophecies of Revelation for God declares the prophecies of the end from the beginning. The following scriptures reveal some of the signals and signs God gives us for the end of the age.

In contrast, anyone who takes away from the words of this book about prophecy, God will take away his part of the Book of Life. You can begin to see how important it is for us to know Jesus; to learn about Him; to love and trust Him with our whole existence so we can spend eternity with Him. If you choose not to, **Revelation 21:8** *"But the cowardly, unbelieving, abominable, murderers, sexually immoral, sorcerers (witches & wizards), idolaters (worshipers of idol objects like statues, money, television, video games) and all liars shall have their part in the lake which burns with fire and brimstone, which is the second death."* Please take note in this last paragraph that the "cowardly" and the "unbelieving" fall into the same category as murderers, sexually immoral and liars. Folks, this is serious stuff!

"Behold, the day of the Lord comes, cruel, with both wrath and fierce anger, to lay the land desolate; and He will destroy its sinners from it. For the stars of heaven and their constellations will not give their light; the sun will be darkened in its going forth, and the moon will not cause its light to shine." **(Isaiah13:9-10)**

"And I will show wonders in the heavens and in the earth: Blood and fire and pillars of smoke. The sun shall be turned into darkness, and the moon into blood, Before the

41

coming of the great and awesome day of the Lord."
(Joel 2:30-31)

"Multitudes, multitudes in the valley of decision! For the day of the Lord is near in the valley of decision. The sun and moon will grow dark, and the stars will diminish their brightness.   *(Joel 3:14-15)*

"Nation will rise against nation, and kingdom against kingdom. And there will be great earthquakes in various places, and famines and pestilences; and there will be fearful sights and great signs from heaven."
(Luke 21:10-11)

"And there will be signs in the sun, in the moon, and in the stars and on the earth distress of nations, with perplexity, the sea and the waves roaring; men's hearts failing them from fear and the expectation of the things which are coming on the earth, for the powers of the heavens will be shaken. Then they will see the Son of Man coming in a cloud with power and great glory. Now when these things begin to happen, look up and lift up your heads, because your redemption draws near."   *(Luke 21:25)*

"I looked when He opened the sixth seal, and behold, there was a great earthquake; and the sun became black as sackcloth of hair, and the moon became like blood." "For the great day of His wrath has come, and who is able to stand?"
(Revelation 6:12, 17)

God reveals His will in many ways. Prophetic words, parables, analogies, and poetry are some examples. In Ezekiel's case, God caused him to see vivid mental pictures---visions of what God was going to do! The Lord Jesus Himself spoke of the wisdom of discerning the signs of the times and of taking appropriate action as we wait for His return.

Matthew 16:2, 3: *"When it is evening ye say it will be fair weather for the sky is red. And in the morning it will be foul weather for the sky is red and lowering. Oh ye hypocrites, ye can discern the face of the sky, but can ye not discern the SIGNS of the TIMES?"*

From the Old Testament to the New Testament we see God using the sun, moon, and stars as "signs" and "signals" for the coming of the Son of Man. There is great power as the earth distresses with earthquakes and the sea roars. There are famines or shortages of food causing starvation and pestilences resulting in pandemics, deadly diseases, viruses and plagues. There will be fearful sights as never seen before and great signs from heaven. God has prophesized by stating in advance what will happen in the future. God is and has always been in complete control of the heavens (sun, moon, and stars) and He numbers our days here on Earth. One of the most supernatural scriptures in the Bible is Matthew 24:29-30:

"Immediately after the tribulation of those days the sun will be darkened, and the moon will not give its light; the stars will fall from heaven, and the powers of the heavens will be shaken. Then the sign of the Son of Man will appear in heaven, and then all the tribes of the earth will mourn, and they will see the Son of Man coming on the clouds of heaven with power and great glory."
(Matthew 24:29-30)

It is hard for us to wrap our minds around this kind of supernatural event, but the Bible states it as truth; therefore, we need to keep looking UP, for the signs of the end times are right out our windows and back door. I will repeat this many times throughout the chapters, "*no one knows the day or hour that the Son of God will return; nor the angels of heaven, or even Jesus himself, only His Father knows for sure.*" Jesus makes it very clear in several passages that no one knows when He will return to set up His kingdom; Jesus himself does not know; only His Father knows **(Mark 13:32; Matthew 24:36)**. Many people may come in His name declaring they know the date Christ will return, but it is untrue, they do not know! What God does ask us to do is: BE WATCHFUL, BE ALERT and BE ON GUARD!

Luke 21:36 "*Watch therefore and pray always that you may be counted worthy to escape all these things that will come to pass, and to stand before the Son of Man.*"

This takes us to the Four Blood Moons occurring in the heavens right now in the years 2014-2015. As of this writing, we have just experienced the third blood moon on April 4, 2015. The last and fourth blood moon is scheduled to happen on September 28, 2015. Many Christians are being WATCHFUL as we observe these moons and how the history of past blood moons have related to events concerning Jews and/or Israel. I am **not** saying that this is the "end of the world" or "the Son of Man coming". This is a time to be WATCHFUL and BE ALERT as this rare phenomenon appears in our skies. Is God trying to give us a WARNING or a "signal" of what is to come? Stay tuned for the next chapter on **"The Four Blood Moons"**.

Therefore, you also be ready, for the Son of Man is coming at an hour you do not expect.
                              (Matthew 24:44)

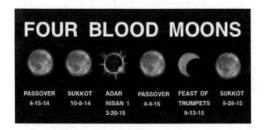

Chapter 3

FOUR BLOOD MOONS

The Four Blood Moons are one of the most compelling wonders of our time. Mark Biltz, founder of El Shaddai Ministries near Seattle, Washington, discovered this amazing series of lunar and solar eclipses that remarkably correspond with God's Hebrew calendar of important the Holy Days of Passover and the Feast of Tabernacles. As we look at the history of the four blood moons; you will be amazed at the accuracy of this new phenomenon. Is God trying to reveal his signs to us? Is He trying to get our attention? Once you read this information, as Joseph Farah states in the foreword section of Mark Biltz's book "Blood Moon", "it's not a question of **if** these signs will occur. It's not even a question of **when** they will occur. About that there is **no** doubt. The only questions that remain to be answered are: what they mean and whether they are biblical harbingers (warnings) of things to come for the world and for God's people."

The Four Blood Moons is a tetrad or a set of four consecutive "total lunar eclipses" in a row. A total lunar eclipse occurs when the Earth's shadow blocks all the sun's light from directly reaching the Moon's surface and it turns the Moon a blood reddish color. The feast days are either Passover (in March/April) or the first day of the Feast of Tabernacles (Sept/Oct), two of God's Holy Days in the Bible. Sometimes these blood moons are referred to as "biblical blood moons" because they fall on two of God's Holy Days.

During the period of 2014-15, as of the writing of this book, we have already experienced three of the blood moons:

Passover - April 15, 2014
Feast of Tabernacles – October 8, 2014
Passover – April 4, 2015
Feast of Tabernacles – September 28, 2015

Interestingly, the blood moon of September 28, 2015 will be seen fully over Jerusalem and it will be a Super Moon; much larger in size than a normal full moon.

History has a way of repeating itself and as we look at the history of previous blood moons we begin to see a pattern of Jews or Israel being affected in a profound way.

In the last 500 years, there have been three (3) episodes of four blood moon tetrads where the full lunar eclipses occurred on Holy Days. These occurred in the years 1492, 1949 and 1967. This is where two of the blood moons appear on Passover (March/April) and the other two appeared on the Feast of Tabernacles (September/October). History tells us that this is a rare occurrence and to have an episode in 2014-15, we need to pay attention. Let us review the history of previous Four Blood Moons:

Year of 1492   (Four Blood Moons on Holy Days)

We associate this date with Columbus discovering America, but also during this time in 1492, King Ferdinand

and Queen Isabella issued an order of expulsion giving the Jewish population four months to either convert to Catholicism or leave the country. It is estimated that between 165,000 and 400,000 Jews fled the country at this time.

Years of 1949-50   (Four Blood Moons on Holy Days)

This was one of the most pivotal moments in human history when Israel, after 1878 years, was proclaimed a nation on May 14, 1948; although the treaty was not officially signed until one year later May 11, 1949. The United Nations announced the natural right of the Jewish people to be masters of their own fate and declared the establishment of the Jewish State known as the State of Israel. **Amos 9:15** *"I will plant Israel in their own land, never again to be uprooted from the land I have given them, says the Lord your God."*

Amazingly, **Isaiah's prophecy in 66:8**, written 740 years before the birth of Jesus, declared: *"Who has heard such a thing? What has seen such things happen? Shall the earth be made to give birth in one day? Or shall a nation be born at once? Secular Israel was born that day!*

The Dead Sea Scrolls were also discovered between the years of 1946-1956, which included this four blood moon period. A collection of 981 different texts were located at Khirbet Qumran in the West Bank.

Amos, the prophet said in 9:11-13 that God would restore the land of David (King David ruled Israel from about 1000 years before Christ was born.) The land of David or

Israel was destroyed and has been in ruins the past 2000 years.

Years of 1967-1968 (Four Blood Moons on Holy Days)

On June 7, 1967, Jerusalem was recaptured by Israel as their capital during the Six Day War despite impossible odds. Almighty God helped little Israel fight this war against all logical odds. According to inserts from the website, *Jewish Virtual Library*, "the armies of Egypt, Jordan, Syria, and Lebanon are poised on the borders of Israel ready to face the challenge of "wiping Israel off of the map". Behind them are the armies of Iraq, Algeria, Kuwait, Sudan and the whole Arab nation, along with the Soviet Union.

Arab's leader states, "Our basic objective will be the destruction of Israel." This act will astound the world. On June 5, 1967, little Israel surprised Egypt by destroying 300 of their tanks, a few hours later, Israeli fighters attacked Jordan, Syria and Iraq. By the end of the first day, nearly the entire Egyptian and Jordanian air forces were destroyed as well as half of Syrians. By the end of the six-day war, Israel had recaptured Jerusalem, the Sinai, Golan Heights, Gaza Strip, West Bank and conquered enough territory to triple the size of Israel from 8,000 to 26,000 square miles." I believe God gave us a clear message, "Don't Mess with Israel, My Promised Land."

Years of 2014-15 (Four Blood Moons on Holy Days)

Many people are divided on whether the four blood moons are signs of the end times or have any prophetic importance. I believe the past history is an indicator that something involving Israel or the Jews will happen.

According to author Perry Stone in his book *Deciphering End-Time Prophetic Codes*, it states, "rabbi's place prophetic significance on a total lunar eclipse called a blood moon falling on Jewish festivals. It is considered a bad omen for the Jewish people, including a sign of internal struggle or a foreboding war." The tetrad historically starts with "tears" and ends with "triumph" for Israel. John Hagee told the Blaze, "When you think about the precision that God has to perform in getting the sun, the moon and the earth in perfect alignment and to produce that exactness on Passover and Feast of Tabernacles...the random probability of that just runs off the charts." God controls the universe which includes the sun, moon and earth. Is God trying to send us a prophetic message? God asked us to be watchful! This is one of those times.

"For this is what the LORD Almighty says: *"After the Glorious One has sent me against the nations that have plundered you--for whoever touches you touches the apple of His eye."* **(Zechariah 2:8)**

Update: The 70th Annual Session of the United Nations General Assembly will open on September 15, 2015. Pope Francis will visit the UN on September 25th and address the world leaders on global climate and how it affects our environment. It is also reported that France and other European nations plan to introduce a resolution which gives formal recognition to a Palestinian state. This draft would define Israel's pre-1967 borders as a reference point for talks, but also designate Jerusalem as the capital of both Israel and a Palestinian state and call for a fair solution for Palestinian refugees. The United States has blocked this in past sessions, but there are concerns President Obama has given the green light to file this motion. There is speculation from the White House that this resolution will pass by an overwhelming majority and be binding on the Israeli government. If this resolution passes, it would be signed on September 28, 2015, our last blood moon. Would this be the start of another big conflict in Israel? It is difficult to imagine Israel and the Palestinians sharing the capital of Jerusalem in a peaceful manner.

The fourth blood moon, September 28, 2015, is also the first day of the Feast of Tabernacles, a Jewish holiday of celebration marking the end of the agricultural year; indicating that the harvest is over, when the wine and oil have been gathered and the time of rejoicing has come.

Sadly, American Christians have very little knowledge about the Jewish Holy Days. Jesus was Jewish, yet most Christians, including myself, have never taken the time to learn about these significant fall festivals. You may not believe in divine appointments, but is it possible that Jesus has a few scheduled ones for us that we are unaware of because we don't have adequate knowledge about the Lord's fall feast holy days?

As we review the Lord's spring festivals we find the original Passover was the rehearsal for Christ's crucifixion as He died on Passover. Christ's burial was during Unleavened Bread, and His resurrection occurred during First Fruit; the first three spring festivals of Israel.

Could it be that major prophetic events, such as the Rapture, Beginning of the Tribulation and eventually the second coming of Christ are designed to line up with His fall festivals? These would include The Feast of Trumpets, The Day of Atonement, and The Feast of Tabernacles. We need to learn more about the Hebrew calendar and His fall festivals to be in tune with His scheduled appointments for His people. During ancient Israel the moon cycles determined when the feasts began each season. One amazing aspect of God's prophetic calendar is how major biblical and prophetic events align with the pattern of the seven festivals.

"And the Lord spoke to Moses, saying, speak to the children of Israel, and say to them: 'The feasts of the Lord, which you shall proclaim to be holy convocations, these are My feasts." **(Leviticus 23:1-2)**

The Lord's seven yearly feasts are holy and as noted in Leviticus, My feasts. Here is a simple chart showing each feast, the Jewish month and the Gregorian calendar (our calendar).

FEAST	JEWISH DATE	GREGORIAN
Passover	First month, Nissan 14th day	March/April
Unleavened Bread	First month, Nissan 15-21st days	March/April
First Fruits	First month, day after Sabbath of Unleavened Bread	March/April
Pentecost	Fifty days from First Fruits	May/June
Trumpets	Seventh month, Tishri First Day	September/October
Atonement	Seventh month, Tishri Tenth Day	September/October
Tabernacles	Seventh month, Tishri 15th through 21st days	September/October

Jesus is our Tabernacle, *"The Word became flesh and lived among us" (John 1:14).* The word "lived" or "dwelt" means *"tabernacle".* When you receive Jesus in your heart,

He comes to live inside of you, and you now become a tabernacle or a dwelling place for the Holy Spirit. What you do with this tabernacle affects your entire life and future.

"Then the Lord spoke to Moses, saying, *"Speak to the children of Israel, saying: 'The fifteenth day of this seventh month shall be the Feast of Tabernacles for seven days to the Lord."* **(Leviticus 23:33)**

"And it shall come to pass that everyone who is left of all the nations which came against Jerusalem shall go up from year to year to worship the King, the Lord of Hosts, and to keep the Feast of Tabernacles." **(Zechariah 14:16)**.

Why are the red blood moons significant? The last blood moon of September 28, 2015 appears on the first day of the "Feast of Tabernacles". After reviewing the history of the previous blood moons that occurred on biblical holy days, we can see that during each sequence something important happened to Israel or the Jews (God's chosen people). During the last 500 years, there have been four tetrads appearing on holy days. The last two biblical blood moon tetrads were in 1949-50 and 1967-68, each having to do with Israel becoming a State and the recapturing of Jerusalem. We will not have another one, according to the NASA website, for another 600 years in 2582-83.

We would be wise to acknowledge that our Lord is trying to grab our attention and tell us something BIG is about to happen. The last blood moon will be September 28, 2015. Write it on your calendar and WATCH what happens in the World between now and then. The Lord has asked us to be watchful, be alert, and be on guard! We can rejoice knowing He has it all under control.

There are only three scriptures in the Bible that contain the words, blood and moon together.

Joel 2:31 (God's Spirit Poured Out) *"The sun shall be turned into darkness, And the moon into blood, Before the coming of the great and awesome day of the Lord."*

Act 2:20 (Peter repeats prophet Joel's words) *"The sun shall be turned into darkness, And the moon into blood, Before the coming of the great and awesome day of the Lord."*

Revelation 6:12 (During the Great Tribulation) *"I looked when he opened the sixth seal, and behold, there was a great earthquake; and the sun became black as sackcloth of hair, and the moon became like blood."*

So here we are in 2015 and the question remains, what will happen in Israel during this blood-moon year? We have the last blood moon on September 28, 2015 and if you are reading this after this date you may already know the answer. Will Israel have to *defend herself* once again with all the unrest in the Middle East? Will the United Nations resolution changing borders back to pre-1967 be approved? Will Iran gain access to nuclear bomb material and try to "wipe Israel off the map"? Many see the Lord preparing our world to enter a new zone, a new shift that may possibly begin with Israel. Can it be the world has willfully turned away from our Creator and He, at this critical point in history, is looking down on us through His window in Heaven with a "tear" in his eye?

I believe that our glorious Lord is trying to grab our attention and tell us something historical and BIG is about to happen for Israel and His people. How will America, Israel's closest ally, defend any attack on Israel? We have been a blessed nation throughout the years by supporting God's promised land of Israel. Yet America, over the last fifty years, has taken God out of our schools, out of our families, out of our lives and out of our hearts. God may be about to give America another warning!

> *"The sun shall be turned into darkness*
> *And the moon into blood, Before the*
> *coming of the great and*
> *awesome day of the Lord."*
> **Joel 2:31**

CHAPTER 4

"Look among the nations and watch---
Be utterly astounded!
For I will work a work in your days,
Which you would not believe;
Though it were told you."
(Habakkuk 1:5)

America: Land of the Free, Home of the Brave; God Bless America; I Pledge Allegiance to the Flag of the United States of America; One Nation, Under God; and In God We Trust. We hear these words in our national anthem, our songs at sporting events, rodeos, parades, and in our breathtaking military songs.

America is considered the land of the free because of the brave 1.3 million men and women who gave their lives defending America. America is free because of the millions, upon millions of veterans who served their country. America is free because of the men and women who are casualties of wars, losing a leg, both legs, an arm, an eye, experiencing shrapnel injuries, brain injuries and the millions who experience PTSD, Post-Traumatic Stress Disorder. Veterans gave their time, their lives, their body parts, and their minds as they once knew it, to the cause of "freedom". We give

55

thanks to all the mothers, fathers, wives, husbands, children and other relatives, who gave up precious time with their veteran, to keep the home front alive as they waited for their return. Our founding fathers of 1776 guaranteed our "inalienable rights" of free speech, free association, freedom to bear arms, and many more. These were derived from God, not granted by government; that all men are created equal and had the precious rights of life, liberty and the pursuit of happiness. As Thomas Jefferson once said, "A government big enough to give you everything you want, is big enough to take away everything you have."

In America are we guilty of pursuing happiness through material items such as houses, second homes, recreational vehicles, cars, boats, larger paychecks, and nice retirements at the expense of our loving God who blesses us with everything we have and own. Are we guilty of forgetting about our loving Father, God & His son, Jesus, who died on the cross for us? Who died with His body and blood to save and forgive us from our sin? Have we forgotten to give Him thanks for everything we own and have in life? Have we forgotten to worship, respect, and honor Him in a way that glorifies only Him?

Let's take a look at the real America that we live in and take a look at what has morally happened to our nation:

- We have taken God and prayer out of the schools and other public places.
- We have removed the Ten Commandments from public places and schools.
- We have taken the word "Jesus" out of most military prayers.
- We can't say the "Pledge of Allegiance" in most schools.
- We no longer say "In God We Trust and God Bless You", when we give a military flag to a mother/wife of a deceased soldier.

- We have removed "In God We Trust" from some coins.
- Family structure has changed through divorce and deterioration of marriage vows.
- More babies are born into single family households.
- Since 1973, through Roe & Wade, we have given permission to abort and kill over 56 million babies.
- Men now have the right to marry men; women have the right to marry women in every State across the nation. (Supreme Court ruling 2015)
- We don't trust in God as a nation; America has become the almighty one. We as a society make our own moral rules.
- Out of 340 million Americans, 73% identify themselves as Christians, but sadly approximately only 20-30% are loyal believers exemplified by following Jesus, worshiping Him, reading the Bible regularly, and attending a place of worship on a regular basis.

As we look at this list, we can't help but realize how morally decayed America has become since about the 1960's as we have taken God out of our lives and replaced Him with our own rules and rights. Let's take a closer look at some of these matters.

Since the 1960's, the family structure has seen many changes. According to the American Psychological Association, marriage is still considered to be healthier and happier for couples and their children, even though the divorce rate is estimated to be 50%. With remarriage and subsequent relationships, the divorce rate climbs to a much higher percentage of about 80%. Single parenting has become more of the norm than in past generations.

In 1973, America passed Roe vs Wade giving women the "right" to abort their unborn child. I believe there are certain circumstances where abortions are warranted, but 56 million! We talk about Hitler killing 6 million Jews in the 1940s; how horrible it was and we mourn for those who lost their lives; yet, we are dead silent when it comes to aborting 56 million babies here in America. God's sixth commandment is "you shall not kill". (Exodus 20:13)

Recently, in our local newspaper, an article was published about "Destigmatizing Abortion". Carol Orr, local resident, wrote an editorial stating, "the first thing I noticed was the picture of a lovely couple with lovely smiles saying 'come on in'; it is okay to take a life and do it without any qualms. Evil comes in many different faces. The couple is selling abortions in a "spa-like" environment. It's fresh, it's modern, it's clean, and it's caring. Notice that they never say what "it" really is---an abortion".

For the Christian; especially the older generation, seeing the decline of morals and values in the United States is painful to watch. It also hurts our Lord. After all, He gave His life for us, so we may be forgiven and repent of our sins. It is so simple, all we have to do is love Jesus with all our heart, our mind and our soul and we can have the kingdom and spend eternity with Him. Yet, so many people in the world today do not understand this simple message. We live in a "self" oriented society and whatever feels good is the "thing" to do instead of the **right thing** by being obedient to God. Unfortunately, they have lots of company around them, so it is easier to take the wide road instead of the narrow road to our Lord Jesus Christ.

Regardless of what God says (Romans 1:18-32) about same-sex marriage, this phenomenon has seemed to grip the nation with the Supreme Court voting, in June 2015, to approve same-sex marriages throughout the entire 50 States. It is sad among Christians, who understand the truth of the Bible, to watch this phenomenon become another **"right"**, because God is clear in the Book of Romans that people who reject God and His standards and practice such "vile passions" are deserving of death. Yes, they can repent, be forgiven, be restored and saved, and receive God's salvation of eternal life, but many refuse to look at God's truth and march for their **"rights"** to do what pleases them.

There is no clearer New Testament reference to the sin of homosexual conduct than this scripture: *"For this reason God gave them up to vile passions. For even their women exchanged the natural use for what is against nature. Likewise also the men, leaving the natural use of the woman, burned in their lust for one another, men with men committing what is shameful and receiving in them the penalty of their error which was due. And even as they did not like to retain God in their knowledge, God gave them over to a debased mind, to do those things which are not fitting"...* **(Romans 1:26-28)**

Regardless of how we feel about divorce, abortion, or same-sex marriage, God asked us in Romans 2 to **NOT** judge or condemn anyone for their actions for those who judge will ALSO be condemned. God's judgment and wrath will prevail. We are all sinners; we are incapable as humans to do what is right all the time. Regardless of how hard we try, we will sin! A sin is a sin no matter what form it takes: from murder, stealing, using God's name in vain, anger, bitterness, turning away from God or dishonoring parents. We need God's help by humbly turning to Him; seeking Him; not by arrogant thinking that we can do it ourselves.

When we disconnect from God, we begin the slippery slope of losing our moral values and our respect for one another. We see on the news many incidents of lawlessness around our nation. With the high use of drugs and alcohol in our nation, crimes are easily committed without regard for the law or respect for authority. When law enforcement attempts to stop the criminal, they resist arrest and then the inevitable happens; someone gets badly hurt or killed. It is sad to watch! The youth have lost respect for the law and the law has lost respect for the criminal. Lawlessness may begin to increase as law enforcement stands down; afraid to do their jobs in fear of constant retaliation from the public, the news departments and the courts.

In the book of **Daniel, Prophecy of the End Time, verse 12:2** says, *"Any many of those who sleep in the dust of the earth shall awake, some to everlasting life, some to shame and everlasting contempt."* **Verse 12:10** goes on to say, *"Many shall be purified, made white, and refined, but the wicked shall do wickedly; and none of the wicked shall understand, but the wise shall understand."*

America has also experienced the rapid development of electronic technology. The prophet **Daniel 12:4** says, *"but you, Daniel, shut up the words, and seal the book until the time of the end; many shall run to and fro, and knowledge shall increase."* Our technological world is working at a pace that is difficult to keep up with as it changes from year to year. It is no wonder that all these earthly signs are developing at a speed faster than we can comprehend. Life as we know it will become more and more chaotic as we experience the end of the age. Natural Disasters will intensify and increase in frequency. The threat of nuclear invasion is always a possibility. Many believe that a nuclear missile would probably be aimed at a high population city such as New York, Washington DC, Los Angeles, Chicago, Seattle, or Houston. The loss or damage of our electromagnetic fields would cause major power outages, affecting most businesses and homes, plus affect our availability to get food and water. If you add the threat of ISIS to our homeland security, you have a recipe for chaos and unrest throughout America. But there is hope among the chaos for you to have everlasting life and that is through Jesus Christ.

ARE WE SAFE FROM TERRORISM?

I wish we could all scream: Wake up America! A majority of Americans seem to be fast asleep; not aware of the dangers that surround us as a nation. Islamic Terrorism is a global threat to our whole world; yet Americans think that the Islam Revolution is just a Middle East or European problem. The general mindset is that ISIS is not here in America fighting, so why worry. Unfortunately, the ultimate goal of Islam is to capture the West and America.

The followers of this militant brand of Islam believe that their God, Allah, has commanded them to conquer the nations of the world both by cultural invasion and by the sword, so what does this mean? We have seen on the news how the "sword" is used for beheadings, killing innocent men, women and children. The cultural invasion is more peaceful where thousands of Muslim families move into a foreign land, build mosques, and attempt to change the culture from the inside out. Normally, they refuse to intermingle with the people of the land, but maintain their own village or community and stay primarily to themselves.

In this quiet fashion, they can conquer the land for Islam. It is being carried out in various places all over the world and throughout the United States.

According to Global Religious Landscape, a report from Pew Research Center dated December 2012; there are an estimated 1.6 billion or 23% of Muslims around the world, making Islam the world's second-largest religious tradition after Christianity. Unfortunately, they are not interested in political solutions. Mr. Walid Shoebat, author of "*God's War on Terror*" and a converted Muslim to Christian states: "They understand only one thing: Their God, Allah, wants total and complete conquest for one religion. Anyone who does not convert to their faith will be executed. This is very dangerous for this is an ideology of hate and revenge and taught to them from birth." This ideology will continue to spread like an out-of-control disease in the years ahead.

Americans do not seem to take this threat very seriously. Sadly, most Americans don't even realize what is happening to their nation. As long as they are fed a constant diet of mindless entertainment, most Americans are perfectly content to let the government and military do their thinking for them. They continue life as they know it and most of the country remains dead asleep. Are we about to receive a wake-up call?

Interestingly enough, people are also talking and expressing concern about Jade Helm, a first-time movement of military vehicles and equipment throughout the nine States of Colorado, Texas, California, Utah, Arizona, Nevada, New Mexico, Mississippi and Florida. The U.S. Army is conducting unique military training exercises throughout these nine states. Questions are being asked by many about the significance of this action by the military and federal government. Are we getting ready for unrest here in

America? Are we preparing for an invasive, take-over by a foreign country or a swarm of natural disasters? At this point, people can only offer speculation.

Christians around America need to be ready to stand firm for Jesus. God needs us to put our armor on and get ready to defend Him. Mr. Walid Shoebat goes on to say, "I am convinced God is looking for 'crazies' who trust in Him. For Moses to take a million Jews and march them through the Red Sea was crazy. Yet Moses trusted in God. For David to challenge Goliath was crazy. Yet David trusted in God. For Israel to enter the Promised Land and fight the giants was crazy. Yet they trusted in God. For Christ to carry His cross was crazy. Yet He trusted in His Father. How stubborn and crazy are you for God?"

It is easy, as Christians, to attend church, sing worship songs, read our Bible, listen to sermons, participate in a few volunteer projects and then go home and do nothing more! I believe Jesus is calling us to do more. He needs to hear our passion and stand up for Him. He will return to rule His kingdom as a roaring lion ready to judge the world. Are we crazy enough as Christians to defend Him against any evil that may exist?   What can we do to encourage non-believers that the Lord is coming and they need to be ready?

"Finally, be strong in the Lord and in His mighty power. Put on the full armor of God that you can take your stand against evil when it comes!"

"Therefore, put on the full armor of God, so that when the day of evil comes, you may be able to stand your ground. In addition, take up the shield of faith....pray in the Spirit on all occasions with all kinds of prayers and requests. With this in mind, be ALERT and always keep on praying for all the saints."

"Pray also for me that whenever I open my mouth, words may be given me so that I will fearlessly make known the mystery of the gospel."
(Ephesians 6:10-11, 13, 18-19)

The rise of radical Islam changed the lives of every American with the tragic event of September 11, 2001; the fall of the World Trade Centers, the damage to the Pentagon and the downing of Flight 93. We experience it every time we wait in an airport security line; every time we hear news of yet another ISIS attack; every time we hear of another beheading; and every time we hear of another American arrested for plotting terrorism activities. It is difficult to wrap our minds around the type of evil we hear about every evening. Most of us just don't know what to do except bury our heads in the sand or change the channel.

In America today, we have financial bedlam with 18 trillion dollars in debt. According to CNN Money, "at the end of July 2013 foreign holders of U.S. Treasury securities totaled close to $5.6 trillion." The top two countries America owes money to are China and Japan:

China	$1.28 Trillion
Japan	1.14 Trillion
Caribbean Bankers	288 Billion
Oil Exporters	258 Billion
Brazil	256 Billion
Taiwan	186 Billion
Switzerland	178 Billion
Belgium	168 Billion
UK	157 Billion
Russia	132 Billion
Hong Kong	120 Billion
Ireland	118 Billion

Canada	65 Billion
Mexico	63 Billion
Germany	56 Billion
Australia	33 Billion
23 Other Countries	967 Billion

As of January 8, 2015, according to the United States National Debt website, the national debt is at 18.1 trillion. "The current debt ceiling suspension expired on March 15, 2015, but the government will likely be able to continue operating through the fall of 2015, using "extraordinary measures" to allow additional borrowing. It is unclear exactly when the money will run out, but sooner or later, lawmakers will have to deal with it."

The existence of thousands of nuclear weapons continues to pose a serious threat to the United States. Nine countries are known to possess nuclear weapons: China, France, India, Israel, North Korea, Pakistan, Russia, UK, and the United States. According to Nuclear Threat Initiative (NTI), a nonprofit organization with a mission to strengthen global security, "It is estimated that these countries collectively hold over 17,300 nuclear warheads. The United States and Russia possess approximately 94% of the world's nuclear weapons." In addition, Iran and Syria are suspected of pursuing nuclear weapon capabilities.

From the Book of Luke, at the end of time, the universal heavens will be shaken as strange, cosmic activity is witnessed by those on earth. The Greek word for great is "mega" which describes an event that is so big that it cannot be ignored as everyone on earth will be a witness. There will also be fearful times when people are frightened and filled with terror.

John, in the book of **Revelation 8:10-12** observed a large asteroid striking the planet creating global panic.

There are a multitude of youtube.com and internet sites discussing an asteroid or meteorite hitting the earth on or about September 24, 2015. Most of them say the government is keeping it quiet to avoid panic among the population. As of the publishing of this book, I was unable to confirm this with NASA. Some of the internet sites are saying that retired NASA employees know this information, but have been told to keep it quiet, but please check out the websites for yourself before making a definite decision on whether this is true or not.

Scientists and astronomers continue to observe the sun and its electromagnetic danger as solar flares 'dance' across the face of the sun. These flares could someday knock out satellites; knocking out or impacting our communication system here on earth. The signs of the sun include solar flares; the signs of the stars include meteorite showers, asteroids and comets; the signs of the moon include lunar eclipses.

We can't help but notice the increase in extreme weather events. The National Climatic Data Center (NCDC) reports, "from 2010-2014, across the United States, there were 4 drought events, 7 flooding events, 30 severe storm events, 4 tropical cyclone events, 2 wildfire events and 2 winter storm events with losses **exceeding $1 billion each**." This does not count the great number of storms resulting in damages under $1 billion.

We have so many unexplained bird and fish deaths in various parts of the United States and the world. If you were to go on the internet and search "unexplained bird and fish deaths", you will be stunned by the actual number of events. In March 2015 alone, there were 92 events of unexplained bird and fish deaths around the globe.

"Hear the word of the Lord, you children of Israel, For the Lord brings a charge against the inhabitants of the land: "There is no truth or mercy or knowledge of God in the land. By swearing and lying, killing and stealing and committing adultery, they break all restraint, with bloodshed upon bloodshed. Therefore the land will mourn; and everyone who dwells there will waste away, with the beasts of the field and the birds of the air; even the fish of the sea will be taken away.   ***(Hosea 4:1-3)***

No matter how terrifying our world may become, it is important that we keep our eyes on Jesus. We must look to the Lord for answers, live for the Lord as if we "belong" to Him and "follow" Him when He whispers to us.

What signs or signals is the Lord giving America? In September 2015, we end another seven-year cycle of the Sabbath. Let's take a look at the history of those cycles and see how they have affected America in the past. You will be shocked to learn the Lord has been warning us for years and He may be about to warn us once again. We need to have our eyes wide open and be watchful.

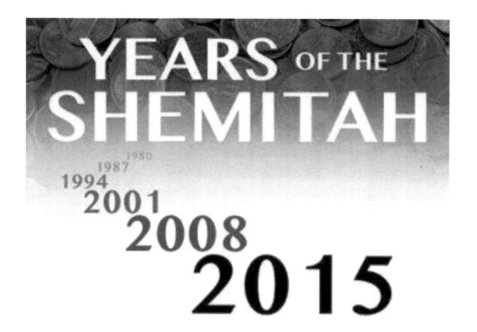

"And at the end of every seven years you shall grant a release of debts. And this is the form of the release: Every creditor who has lent anything to his neighbor shall release it; he shall not require it of his neighbor or his brother, because it is called the Lord's release."

(Deuteronomy 15:1-2)

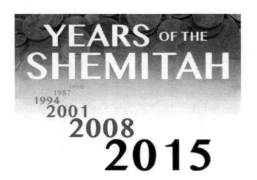

CHAPTER 5

WARNING AMERICA:

THE SEVEN YEAR "SHEMITAH"

Bestselling author, Jonathan Cahn, Senior Rabbi at the nation's largest messianic congregation, the Beth Israel Worship Center in Wayne, N.J., has written two books, "*The Harbinger*" and "*The Mystery of the Shemitah*", which are well worth reading. I highly recommend them for a thorough presentation of the mysterious warnings the Lord is showing to America. Rabbi Cahn uses the Hebrew word, *Shemitah,* which means "wiping away of debts, a cleansing, a releasing of debt, or a canceling of debt." In this brief chapter, I will not attempt to explain the nine harbingers or warnings that Rabbi Cahn explains in his book, *The Harbinger*, but I do recommend reading the book for your own insights. It will change your world!

Jonathan Cahn writes in his new book "The Mystery of the Shemitah, "Is it possible that the words of an ancient text are determining and controlling the future of the financial realm, the business realm, and the economic realm?" This is an amazing phenomenon that every American should pay attention to as we look into the greatest overall collapses and stock market crashes and find a 3,000 year old mystery that determines a pattern matching a specific seven year cycle of the biblical Sabbath that is described in the Bible. This is not about setting a date and waiting for something to happen. The most important thing, no matter what happens, is to be right with God and know He is in full control. Like Mr. Cahn says, "Are there signs and harbingers warning us of what lies ahead? Is America in danger of a coming calamity, a collapse, even God's judgment for turning away from Him"?

It is hard to believe, but if you were to do research on the past 40 years of American history on peaks and collapses of economic downfalls, you will begin to see the seven year cycle emerge. In other words, every seven years, America has experienced an event that has caused a wiping away or release of debt in our economy and in our financial markets. As you read the following scriptures from the Old Testament, keep in mind that the Feast of Tabernacles is always in September/October on our Gregorian calendar.

"And at the end of every seven years you shall grant a release of debts. And this is the form of the release: Every creditor who has lent anything to his neighbor shall release it; he shall not require it of his neighbor or his brother, because it is called the Lord's release."

(Deuteronomy 15:1-2)

Then Moses commanded them: "At the end of every seven years, in the year for canceling debts, during the Feast of Tabernacles, when all Israel comes to appear before the Lord your God at the place he will choose, you shall read this law before them in their hearing. Assemble the people, men, women and children, and the aliens living in your towns, so they can listen and learn to fear the Lord your God and follow carefully all the words of this law.
(Deuteronomy 31:10-12)

The shocker is that beginning in 1973, every single one of the five greatest financial peaks and collapses have taken place during the set time of the Shemitah, every "seven" years. The number "7" has significant value in the Bible and is the number of **completeness and perfection**. It originates much of its meaning from being attached directly to God's creation of all things. Just as God created the heavens and the earth in six days, He blessed the seventh day and made it holy, because on it he rested from all the work of creating that he had done.

"Thus the heavens and the earth were completed in all their vast array. By the seventh day God had finished the work he had been doing; so on the seventh day he rested from all his work. And God blessed the seventh day and made it holy, because on it he rested from all the work of creating that he had done." **(Genesis 2:1-3)**

The number "7" is used approximately 735 times in the Bible and in the **Book of Revelation** alone it is used 54 times. There are seven days in a week; God's Sabbath is on the 7th day; there are seven churches, seven seals, seven trumpet plagues, seven thunders, seven lampstands, seven bowls, and the Bible was originally divided into seven divisions. They are the Law, the Prophets, the Psalms, the Gospels and Acts, the General Epistles or Letters, the Letters of Paul, and the Book of Revelation. The first resurrection of the dead takes place at the 7th trumpet, completing salvation for the Church.

There are seven annual Holy Days connected to God's annual Feast Days, beginning with Passover and ending with the Feast of Tabernacles in the fall. These Holy Days consist of Passover and Feast of Unleavened Bread, Feast of First Fruits, Feast of Weeks or Pentecost, Feast of Trumpets, Day of Atonement, and Feast of Tabernacles, which ends in the 7th month of the Hebrew Calendar, Tishri.

In addition to a Sabbath Day of rest, Israel observes a Sabbath year, the seventh year of solemn rest for the land to remind the people of Israel that their land was a gift from the Lord and ultimately belonged to Him.

The Lord spoke to Moses on Mount Sinai, saying, "Speak to the children of Israel and say to them: 'When you come to the land which I give you, then the land shall keep a Sabbath to the Lord. Six years shall you sow your field, and six years you shall prune your vineyard, and gather its fruits; but in the seventh year there shall be a Sabbath of solemn rest for the land, a Sabbath to the Lord.'"

(Leviticus 25:1-4)

Throughout the Bible there are many references to the number "7"; God's number for completeness and perfection. There many references to the Sabbath and the cycle of seven years. The Bible reveals in many ancient stories that God warns before judgment. God sends warnings through visions, dreams, voices, prophecy, supernatural occurrences, through unusual weather events and through the sun, moon and the stars. The Bible is clear that *"God does not change for He is Lord" and says "Return to Me, and I will return to you."* **(Malachi 3:6-7)**

Let's get back to the Shemitah or Sabbath years here in America, and take a look at the history that has happened here in the United States. One of the big questions is, as we looked at the loss of morality in America in the previous chapter, are we about to receive another warning from God? We have taken God out of so many aspects of our society; therefore, could we as a Nation be about to receive another warning?

The seventh year of this cycle is known as the Year of the Shemitah and runs from September 2014 to September 13, 2015. It ends on the last day of the 6th month of the Hebrew calendar, Elul 29. The last day of Elul 29 is the peak and accumulation of the whole year as the year builds up to that final day when everything is released and wiped away in one day. This Hebrew date of Elul 29 is a different date on our Gregorian calendar. It usually appears sometime in September but on different dates each year due to lunar movements. The most important aspect of this paragraph is to remember Elul 29 as it will come up again and again in this chapter.

For those believers or followers of God, the Shemitah year can also be a year of abundance since the Shemitah belongs to God. God is absolute and supreme. The realm of money, finances, economies and our possessions are under man's keeping, but ultimately belong to God alone. He is first and foremost above all these commodities. God can cleanse and wipe away all excesses, which build up over the seven years. What we have encountered in America is a massive cleaning of our financial and economical accounts when people or governments do not follow God. God is warning us as judgment day nears!

Let's now take a look at what has happened in the United States during the past four Shemitahs, the seven year cycles. You may find that some of these events did not affect you personally; it all depends on your spiritual, financial and economic situation. The following information has all been verified by research of various sources from the Internet.

SHEMITAH YEAR 1986-87

On October 19, 1987, Black Monday erupted with a stock market fall of 508 points wiping away 22.6% of the value of stocks. This was considered to be the first global financial crisis on a day known as "**Black Monday**." According to the Federal Reserve Bank, "A chain reaction of market distress sent global stock exchanges plummeting in a matter of hours. In the United States, the DOW dropped 22.6% in a single trading session, a loss marking the sharpest market downturn in the United States since the Great Depression."

This event happened on the Hebrew calendar date of Tishri 26, or October 19, 1987; on the year of the Shemitah.

SHEMITAH YEAR 1993-1994

The United States experienced the worst bond market fall in history after a sharp unexpected increase in interest rates. Fortune website reports, "The Federal Reserve began nudging short-term interest rates higher resulting in the bond market inflicting heavy damage on financial companies, hedge funds and bond mutual funds. Fortune estimates the rise in 30-year interest rates from 6.2% to 7.75% which knocked more than $600 billion off the value of U.S. bonds." Worldwide the decline in bond values was estimated to be on the order of $1.5 trillion. This was considered a surprising and major setback that confounded virtually every major bond investor on Wall Street.

This event gradually happened between the dates of September 5, 1994 and October 3, 1994, which started on Elul 29 and ended on Tishri 28, the year of the Shemitah.

SHEMITAH YEAR 2000-2001

Due to the terrorist attack on the World Trade Centers, the Pentagon, and the downing of Flight 93 in Pennsylvania on September 11, 2001, the market was closed and reopened on September 17, 2001 to one of history's largest point drops. The market dropped 684.81 points, or 7.13% of the market down to the DOW of 8,920.70. Major stock sell-offs hit the airline and insurance companies. Hardest hit were American Airlines and United Airlines, the planes that were hijacked for the terrorist attacks. American Airlines closed on September 17 to a 39% decline and United Airlines dropped 42%. Other declines hit the travel, tourism, hospitality, entertainment and financial services companies as a wave of panic and uncertainty swept through America. Insurance firms eventually paid out an estimated $40 billion in 9/11 related claims. Many investors claim to have lost a value of 40-50% of their stocks or mutual funds during this time.

This event happened on September 17, 2001, exactly on the Hebrew date of Elul 29, the last day of the year of the Shemitah. Notice that the warnings are getting bigger and more intense on each seven-year cycle.

SHEMITAH YEAR 2007-2008

On September 29, 2008, a global financial crisis resulted in Wall Street falling 777.7 points or 7% of the total market. According to CNN Money, "Stocks skidded in the biggest single-day point loss ever, after the House rejected the government's $700 Billion bank bailout plan. The day's loss knocked out approximately $1.2 Trillion in market value."

The Federal Reserve and other central banks around the world announced that they would make billions of dollars available to troubled banks:

-Citigroup bought Wachovia's bank assets of $2.2 billion and absorbed their losses of $42 billion. JP Morgan Chase bought Washington Mutual after it suffered the largest failure ever as a US bank. JP Morgan shares immediately fell 15%.

-Fannie Mae and Freddie Mac voluntarily went into conservatorship as they recognized their losses were coming from taxpayer money. It appeared that the collapse of the housing credit bubble was an event that caused the failure of Fannie Mae and Freddie Mac.

-Other banks suffered as National City lost 63%, Bancorp fell 43% and Regions Financial 41%. Goldman Sachs, Merrill Lynch and Bank of American also took big losses. Global markets struggled all over the world from Europe to Asia.

The situations with the banks caused a credit freeze or change with fewer people able to access credit. Foreclosures resulted in over 500 million families or investors losing their homes. In 2008 alone, 2.6 million jobs were lost and the unemployment rate jumped to 7.2%. More than 11 million Americans were unemployed; a dire situation for many America families. This catastrophic event was one of the largest losses the United States has ever experienced and we are still paying for it today.

This event happened on September 29, 2009; the last day of the Hebrew month Elul 29, the year of the Shemitah.

SHEMITAH YEAR 2014-2015

Here we are about to end another Shemitah year in 2015. Two of the last major "releasing of debt" was in 2001 and 2008, both happening exactly on the last day of the Hebrew calendar of the month of Elul 29. Even though September 11, 2001 and September 29, 2008 are not exactly seven years apart on our Gregorian calendar, they are exactly seven years apart on the biblical Hebrew calendar. The other two events were in 1994 and 1987, both happening in and around the same period on the Hebrew calendar.

In 2015, the day of Elul 29 will be September 13th on our Gregorian calendar. This happens to be a Sunday so we know the stock market will not fall on a Sunday because Wall Street is closed. If history is to repeat itself, something significant could happen around September 13 to October 11, 2015 that could affect our financial and economic world where accounts are once again wiped clean or transformed.

Please note that this is not the author setting dates, it is what history has shown us.

Our nation has continued to turn away from God as a whole so the question remains: "Are we about to encounter another warning from God?" Past history shows us God's judgment.

When you add the rare phenomenon of the four blood moons appearing in 2014-2015 with the last blood moon appearing on September 28, 2015 and the Year of the Shemitah being 2014-15, we can't help but want to pay attention. Wake-up America, for God has asked us to BE WATCHFUL, BE ALERT and BE ON GUARD, for we do not know when He will come like a thief in the night.

Billy Graham is, (in an interview with award-winning journalist Troy Anderson) one of the most admired men in the World, and he states, "This is an exciting and thrilling time to be alive. The Apocalypse (the unveiling of the end times) speaks of powerful troubles ahead with storm warnings that carry a booming jolt of truth. A new world is coming! Christ is coming to conquer evil and establish his perfect rule over all creation. But until then God wants to give everyone an opportunity to know Christ through repentance and faith. It is time to return to biblical truth."

Luke 9:56: *"For the Son of Man did not come to destroy men's lives but to save them."*

Matthew 5:17: *"Do not think that I came to destroy the Law or the Prophets. I did not come to destroy but to fulfill."*

Matthew 5:16: *"Let your light so shine before men, that they may see your good works and glorify your Father in Heaven."*

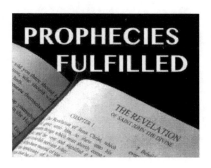

CHAPTER 6

DISCOVERING PROPHECY

According to Tim LaHaye, co-author of the *Left Behind* series and co-author, Thomas Ice, of the book, *"Charting the End Times,"* "The Bible is the only source of dependable prophetic truth. A prophet is defined as 'one who speaks on behalf of another,' and a prophecy is the message that he reveals. The Bible is a detailed roadmap of future events to happen. Bible prophecy is God's message to man, spoken and written by prophets specially chosen by God, hundreds of years ago. Today, many people think prophecy deals only with predictions about the future, but that is not the case. The Lord determines what will happen in history and then He brings it to pass." "Prophecy is history written in advance."

"Behold, the former things have come to pass, And new things I declare; Before they spring forth I tell you of them."   **(Isaiah 42:9)**

"But all this was done that the Scriptures of the prophets might be fulfilled."   **(Matthew 26:56)**

For example, the Lord said through Isaiah the prophet,

> *"Remember the former things, those of long ago;*
> *I am God, and there is no other;*
> *I am God, and there is none like me.*
> *I make known the end from the beginning, from ancient*
> *times, what is still to come.*
> *I say: My purpose will stand, and I will do all that I please.*
> *From the east I summon a bird of prey;*
> *from a far-off land, a man to fulfill my purpose.*
> *What I have said, that will I bring about;*
> *what I have planned, that will I do."*
> **(Isaiah 46:9-11, NIV)**

Christianity is developed upon God's revelation of Himself to mankind as found in the Bible. How can we trust that prophecy is not just man's interpretation of historical biblical events? Many of the prophecies of the Bible were written hundreds of years before the actual event, so we begin to see that in the Old Testament, before Christ was born, that it was prophesized in **Micah 5:2** that the birth of a Messiah would happen in Bethlehem. This was estimated to be written between 735-700 B.C.; before Christ was born. How is a prophecy different from a prediction? A prediction made by man is just a guess and may or may not come true; a prediction of God is given from His foreknowledge of future events and will come true. When God communicates His prophetic message through an individual, this person is being used as a prophet of God. Thus one of the tests of a true prophet of God is 100% accuracy as it speaks to the authority of God's truth and character.

Deuteronomy 18:22 states, "*When a prophet speaketh in the name of the LORD, if the thing follow not, nor come to pass, that is the thing which the LORD hath not spoken, but the prophet hath spoken it presumptuously: thou shalt not be afraid of him.*"

Prophets are often thought of as those who only predict the future, yet this was only a part of their role. They were primarily sent to proclaim God's message, and this was often to denounce sin and warn of coming judgment, the aim of which was to avert this by turning God's people to repentance.

"*And we have the word of the prophets made more certain, and you will do well to pay attention to it, as to a light shining in a dark place, until the day dawns and the morning star rises in your heart.*" **(2 Peter 1:19, NIV)**

"*Above all, you must understand the no prophecy of Scripture came about by the prophet's own interpretation. For prophecy never had its origin in the will of man, but men spoke from God as they were carried along by the Holy Spirit.*" **(2 Peter 1:20-21, NIV)**

Why is it important for Christians to study Biblical Prophecy? Prophecy offers us an overview of God's plan for man in the future. As we study and realize that many of the prophecies have already been fulfilled, we become stronger in our beliefs that God is indeed very real! **Daniel 2:28**, one of the Bible's Major Prophets, *states "but there is a God in heaven who reveals mysteries"*. Another important reason for Christians to study prophecy is to know the teachings of

God's word.   Many false prophets will appear in the end times and the best way to avoid being deceived is to know God's word and know the Scriptures.   God, through prophecy, slowly reveals the mysteries of what is to come; when we need to know it. Therefore, it is important we keep our eyes on what prophecies are being fulfilled so we know the truth.

"Watch out for false prophets.   They come to you in sheep's clothing, but inwardly they are ferocious wolves.
(Matthew 7:15, NIV)

"Jesus answered: "Watch out that no one deceives you, for many will come in my name, claiming, "I am the Christ" and will deceive many". **(Matthew 24:4-5, NIV)**

(During the signs of the end of the age) "And many false prophets will appear and deceive many people". **(Matthew 24:11, NIV)** *"At that time if anyone says to you, 'Look, here is the Christ!' or, "There he is!' do not believe it, for false Christs and false prophets will appear and perform great signs and miracles to deceive even the elect, if that were possible. See, I have told you ahead of time."*
(Matthew 24:23-25, NIV)

Sadly, many pastors and ministers are not teaching prophecy in the church today because either they have received very little training or they do not want to create an atmosphere of fear in their congregation. Therefore, many Christians may not be hearing the Word and the excitement that our Lord is indeed coming and that God has wonderful plans for the future of the believer.

Learning about prophecy, especially those Scriptures that describe our Lord's return actually motivates believers to live a purer life. *"Everyone who has this hope in him purifies himself, just as He is pure."* **(1 John 3:3)**. Christians who believe that the Lord will return at the twinkling of an eye have a desire to keep their lives pure in heart so they are ready for the Lord when he comes. They are not so apt to fall to temptation because the time is near and they want to remain pure in heart.

"Behold, I am coming soon! Blessed is He who keeps the words of the prophecy in this book." **(Revelation 22:7)** Jesus is coming back...it could even be today. Some of His last words recorded in the Bible are *"Surely I am coming quickly."* **(Revelation 22:20)**

There are over 300 prophecies in scripture that Jesus fulfilled at His first coming. Many of these were made sometimes hundreds of years before Jesus was even born. This is why prophecy is an indication of the divine composition of the scriptures, and therefore a testimony to the trustworthiness of the message of the scriptures.

Micah, the prophet, spoke in **Micah 5:2** of the Messiah's birth almost 700 years before He came to life. **Isaiah 7:14** spoke of *"Therefore the Lord Himself will give you a sign: behold, the virgin shall conceive and bear a Son and shall call His name Immanuel."* What is the likelihood of a person today predicting such a profound event as the birth of Christ 700 years in advance? It would be impossible without God's authority and guidance.

Furthermore, Jesus' death was also prophesized in the Bible as He was sneered and mocked. The Book of Psalms was written by about 150 authors over several centuries, but assembled together around 537 BC. Jesus was crucified around April 3, 33 A.D.

"All those who see me ridicule Me; they shoot out the lip, they shake the head, saying, 'He trusted in the Lord, let Him rescue Him; let Him deliver Him, since he delights in him?'"   **(Psalms 22:7,8)**

"And the people stood looking on. But even the rulers with them sneered saying, 'He saved others; let Him save Himself if he is the Christ, the chosen of God.'"

(Luke 23:35)

Prophecies are God's gift to us from the Old Testament to the New Testament to present day. One of the most important prophecies in the Bible is **Daniel 9:24-27** because it gives explicit time frames for the appearance of the Messiah; His death and His return. The timing of His first coming would be exactly 483 years after the issuing of the decree to restore and rebuild Jerusalem. The timing of His second coming will occur exactly seven years after the ruler (antichrist) who will come and confirm a covenant with many. The covenant or treaty will be one that concerns Israel and the rebuilding of the Jewish Temple in Jerusalem. The seven year timeline is called the Tribulation.

Many people ask, "Why would a loving God come to judge us and put us through a wrath of trials?" "God is a loving God and He came to offer us salvation through Jesus, not wrath. The wrath we bring on ourselves is by not believing. Just like an earthly father, we discipline our kids so they will learn the truth. God is doing the same thing, but on a larger scale. **John 12:13** *"Blessed is He who comes in the name of the Lord".*

"For God did not appoint us to wrath, but to obtain salvation through our Lord Jesus Christ."

(1 Thessalonians 5:9)

God is a God of grace and He is a God of love. We have been given over 2000 years of a "grace period" to come to know him. **Daniel 4** confirms that grace has an expiration date, by revealing a prophetic word that was spoken over King Nebuchadnezzar and then in verse 28 says, *"12 months later, an angel spoke the same word to him and immediately the word spoken had come to pass in his life"*.

When Christ's followers or the Church are raptured, the period of grace will expire for those left behind. God wants everyone to repent, come to know Him and restore their faith, but if people refuse to obey during the grace period of the church, then they will be subject to judgment.

He loves us so much that He has given us many years to learn about Him, to fall in love with Him, and to surrender our lives to Him. He wants only goodness for us and to save us. The church is not destined for wrath. It is promised salvation from the wrath to come as in **1 Thessalonians 1:10:** *"to wait for his Son from heaven."* Jesus gave His life for us to save us from sin. He gave his life by being beaten and dying a terrible death on the cross in order to SAVE us, not to judge us. It will only be those who turn away from Jesus who will be subject to the wrath. Remember, it has been prophesized that Jesus was born the sacrificial lamb of the Father, but will return to rule as a lion.

He wants to give us the kingdom, and He will if we can repent of our sins, and humble ourselves before Him. God also gave His one and only Son, Jesus, to be sacrificed on the cross so that we may be forgiven for our sins. His only son, Jesus, sacrificed His body and His blood for us. Humbly, we should all be honored to love Him!

"As for the person who hears my words but does not keep them, I do not judge him, for I did not come to judge the world, but to save it. There is a judge for the one who rejects me and does not accept my words; that very word which I spoke will condemn him at the last day."

(John 12:47)

One of the most profound and important scripture in the Bible is **John 3:16**. For many children this is the first scripture they memorize in Sunday school. It is one that says it all in just a few words. *"For God so loved the world that He gave His one and only Son, that whoever believes in Him shall not perish but have eternal life. For God did not send His Son into the world to condemn the world, but to save the world through Him. Whoever believes in Him is not condemned, but whoever does not believe stands condemned already because he has not believed in the name of God's one and only Son. This is the verdict: Light has come into the world, but men loved darkness instead of light because their deeds were evil. Everyone who does evil hates the light, and will not come into the light for fear that his deeds will be exposed. But whoever lives by the truth comes into the light, so that it may be seen plainly that what he has done has been done through God.* **(John 3:16-21, NIV)**

Dr. David Jeremiah states in *"The Jeremiah Study Bible"*, "Even though it has been over 2,000 years since Christ's first coming or His birth; His second coming is certain. The testimony of Christ's own words in **Matthew 24:30** tells us that Jesus will return to balance the scales of justice, gather His people to Himself in His Kingdom and establish His rightful place as King of Kings and Lord of Lords. It is not a question of whether every knee will bow and every tongue confess that He is Lord---it is only a matter of when." **(Isaiah 45:23; Phil 2:10)**

WHY STUDY PROPHECY?

One reason to study prophecy is that it gives us peacefulness and confidence that God is working out His ultimate plan for the world. This takes away the fear as we watch our unholy world unravel before our eyes. Our Lord Himself warns us that toward the end of human history there would be a time of *"great tribulation, such as has not occurred since the beginning of the world until now, nor ever will". (Matthew 24: 21)* When we understand God's future plan for us, we can rest in his Words and have peaceful confidence. In Revelation, we see that history has an end goal; we see that God is working out His ultimate plan for the world. We can see that God really is in control and that Jesus will ultimately be, *"ruler of all the kings of the earth".*
                                                    (Revelation 1:5)

Another reason to study prophecy is we receive blessings from God by not only reading it, but "hearing" it and taking into our "hearts" what is written. As we watch our immoral world crumble and change before our eyes on national television and knowing most of the prophecies have been fulfilled, we realize that the time is near!

Jesus, Himself, said, "Do not think that I came to destroy the Law or the Prophets. I did not come to destroy but to fulfill."   *(Matthew 5:17)*

"Blessed is the one who reads the words of this prophecy, and blessed are those who hear it and take to heart what is written in it, because the time is near."

(Revelation 1:3)

"Behold, I am coming soon! Blessed is he who keeps the words of the prophecy in this book."

(Revelation 22:7)

You can find encouragement in the law and the prophets, but the only true glory in life and in eternity, is being found in the presence of the Lord Jesus Christ. True joy, fulfillment, and peace in your life come when you have a relationship with Him. Paul said, *"For me to live is Christ but to die is gain"* **(Philippians 1:21)**. This is a two-fold promise. Living every day with Jesus is such a blessing. And knowing that when we die we will be with Him, face-to-face, for eternity is even better! So until we are with Him for eternity, we keep serving Him giving Him all the glory.

Jesus fulfilled everything in the law and everything by the prophets. And Jesus can surely fulfill everything in your life when you surrender it to Him. Paul quoted Habakkuk to support this point that God will judge those who reject Jesus Christ. **(Acts 13:41)** *"Look, you scoffers, wonder and perish, for I am going to do something in your days that you would never believe, even if someone told you."*

Look among the nations and watch—
Be utterly astounded!
For I will work a work in your days
Which you would not believe, though it were told you.

(Habakkuk 1:5)

Jesus warns everyone in **Revelation 22:18-19** that *"everyone who hears the words of the prophecy of this book: If anyone adds anything to them, God will add to him the plagues described in this book, and anyone takes words away from this book of prophecy, God will take away from him his share in the tree of life and in the holy city, which are described in this book."*

Jesus makes it crystal clear in scripture that we are not to add or take away from His Words. The pressure is great for those who hear, write or talk about prophecy, for mistakes can result in his share of the tree of life being removed.

In **Revelation 22:10-13**, Jesus told John, *"DO NOT SEAL UP THE WORDS OF THE PROPHECY OF THIS BOOK, BECAUSE THE TIME IS NEAR. Let him who does wrong continue to do wrong, let him who is vile continue to be vile (disgusting, hateful, evil, dreadful), let him who does right continue to do right and let him who is holy continue to be holy."*

"Behold, I am coming soon! My reward is with me, and I will give to everyone according to what he has done. I am the Alpha and the Omega, the First and the Last, the Beginning and the End." **(Revelation 22:12)**

When Jesus comes again, He will come as the *"King of kings and the Lord of lords"* **(Revelation 19:16)** to once again rule over the nations. King of kings means Jesus is the One who will be 'supreme' over all the earthly kings or rulers and no one will be in a position to challenge His authority. God has given us many prophecies in the Bible to watch for in our current times. Be on guard, for as these prophecies are fulfilled, the mystery will be revealed by the signs of the end times. Most Christians will agree, the time feels more and more urgent and time may be running out. Only God knows for sure. As we look at the world and see prophecies fulfilled, we realize the time of our Lord's return is closer than ever before. Time is getting shorter!

The Word of the Bible answers all of our questions. Please don't be caught sleeping for the time is near!

Jesus is coming back...it could even be today. Some of His last words recorded in the Bible are "Surely I am coming quickly." **(Revelation 22:20)**

It is important to know and it will be stressed many times throughout this book that even though Christians believe with all their hearts that Jesus is coming for the church soon, no one knows the day or the hour, not even Jesus knows, only the Father. Scripture is very clear:

"Remember, No one knows about that day or hour, not even the angels in heaven, nor the Son, but only the Father. Be on guard! Be alert! You do not know when that time will come. He will come in the twinkling of an eye; do not let him find you sleeping. What I say to you, I say to everyone: WATCH!" **(Mark 13:32-37)**

In summary, prophecies of the Bible are told in advance of their happening. Jesus' birth, His teachings, His death, His resurrection, the rapture, the judgments, the tribulation, His second coming and the New Heaven and Earth have all been prophesized. Let's take a brief look at how America fits into prophecy.

> *"Blessed is the one who reads the words of this prophecy, and blessed are those who hear it and take to heart what is written in it, because the time is near."* (Revelation 1:3)

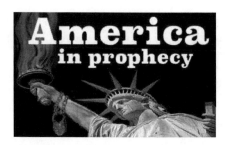

CHAPTER 7

AMERICA IN PROPHECY

"Today, many people think prophecy deals only with predictions about the future, but that is not the case. **Prophecy is history written in advance**. The Lord determines what will happen in history and then He brings it to pass. The Bible is the only source of dependable prophetic truth. God is saying to us through scripture to remember the prophecies of long ago and that He has made known "the end from the beginning" of ancient times and there is no other God. What He has said in the past 'has a purpose' and what He said long ago; He promises to bring the plans to reality.

As we review prophecy do we find America in the Bible? Do we find America functioning during the end times?

America is such a young nation, founded in 1776 and only 239 years old, compared to the Bible written over 2000 years ago. There are various theories regarding references to America in Bible prophecy. While there are no verses directly mentioning America by name, there are a few scriptures that refer to "*the nations*", but there is no clear indication that "the nations" include America.

If America is not in Bible prophecy then we have to ask the question: "Why not?" After all, America has been one of the key players in providing support for Israel since 1948. America through the years has offered financial support to help build and protect Israel. Many other nations are not mentioned in prophecy either; however, it is hard to understand why the world's most powerful nation is not mentioned. America is Israel's closest ally. "*God promises to bless those who bless Israel and curse those who curse Israel.*" **(Genesis 12:3)** America's relationship with Israel will be closely watched.

There are many theories and ideas as to why we are not mentioned, but here are a few ideas based on speculation. We do not know the answers and we must watch and wait to see what God's plan is for America.

- Perhaps America is no longer pertinent or important. Maybe it is destroyed or damaged in such a manner that it is no longer a world power and plays no significant role in God's end-time plans.
- Perhaps America is no longer its own country, but joined with another country or a larger union of countries, and controlled by their leader or the Antichrist. We are in debt to China and Japan for trillions of dollars; can we repay them?
- As we talked in Chapter 1, maybe America goes through a financial crisis and eventually *implodes* within its infrastructure and goes bankrupt. Financially, if American cannot reduce the 18 trillion in debt, we are a sitting target for future disruption in government services, possibly resulting in a federal government shutdown. Credit can only go so far

before we reach its limit. If our federal government was to shut down, many government programs such as Obamacare, Social Security, Medicare, Welfare, food stamps, would be disrupted. This would be a major change in how Americans live and possibly trigger more lawlessness in the fight to survive.

- One serious threat to our country is an electromagnetic pulse attack (EMP). Such an attack would brutally damage all of our electrical power systems, electronic and information system, which would include electric power, computers, mobile phones, cars, airplanes, banking, satellites, fuel, energy, emergency services and our ability to obtain adequate food and water. This type of attack would be very harmful to Americans and take months or even years to fully recover from. If this was to happen today, would you be prepared? This is not meant to scare you, but to be awake, alert and be prepared. In our own household, we have taken some steps to prepare by stocking up on extra dried or canned food, kerosene lanterns, extra drinking water, extra batteries for radio, and a propane cook stove. It is a good idea to be prepared for any emergency that might come our way.

- Update: On June 14, 2015, David Petraeus, former four-star general, who led forces in Iraq and Afghanistan, said in an interview for News.max: "There's no question that the industrial-strength threat emanates from China, adding that Syria and Russia also pose dangers. Operating systems in the U.S. electrical grid and water systems are vulnerable. The federal government needs to spend more to strengthen the cybersecurity of the U.S.

infrastructure." On July 8, 2015, the NY Stock Exchange lost computer power for four hours; unheard of in the history of the stock exchange. On the same day, United Airlines lost their computer power, shutting down the entire United Airline travel for the day. Both were reported as malfunctions; consequently, happening on the same day.

- We are always under the threat of nuclear weapons, especially with North Korea and Russia having weapons ready to aim and fire. We also have the threat of Iran obtaining the means to have active nuclear weapons. Officials state that most likely a nuclear weapon would be directed to one of the larger cities in the United States like New York, Washington DC, Chicago, Los Angeles, San Francisco or Houston.

- According to Ron Rhodes in his book, "*The Popular Dictionary of Bible Prophecy*", he states, "One final reason the United States is not mentioned in Bible prophecy is that it could be affected catastrophically by the rapture. There are more Christians per square mile in the United States than anywhere else on earth." Currently, 340 million Americans or 73% identify themselves as Christians. Of the 73%, estimates believe only 30-40% are loyal believers. Many attend church on occasion or own a bible, but never open it to study the word. Of the 30-40%, there is speculation that fewer than 20% would be raptured or considered "true followers of Jesus Christ". *With these figures there would still be 68 million Americans raptured and vanishing all at once.*

It is fair to say the United States would be negatively impacted and take years to recover. Can you imagine 68 million Americans vanishing from their jobs, homes, businesses, cars, trucks, and planes? There would be extreme chaos throughout the nation with people disappearing into thin air causing accidents, commotion and complete madness. People would be looking for loved ones, unable to imagine that the rapture actually happened. The shock of the reality of the situation would be one big nightmare to discover their loved ones were missing. Then the reality settles in that they were "left behind".

"For the Lord Himself will descend from heaven with a shout, with the voice of an archangel, and with the trumpet of God. And the dead in Christ will rise first. Then we who are alive and remain shall be caught up together with them in the clouds to meet the Lord in the air. And thus we shall always be with the Lord. Therefore comfort one another with these words" **(1 Thessalonians 4:16-17).**

This is either comfort to you, as Paul says, or it's a wake-up call for you. We need to start living with fear, and awe, and respect of God in our lives. He is coming back, and it will be decisive and definite. Are you ready? So often we let our eyes watch things, and we let our minds hear things, and we let our hands handle things, and we let our hearts be exposed to things that are really impure. We lack the fear of God. Recognizing who God truly is puts us in our place. And when we're in that place of reverent fear and submission to His Will, we have peace. We have peace and comfort knowing that He is our God and that He is our Savior. And that is the only way we'll ever find true peace.

Grant Jeffrey, Bible prophecy teacher and author of 30 books, published his last book, *"One Nation, Under Attack: How Big-Government Liberals are Destroying the America*

You Love." He writes, "International financiers and powerful socialist forces are working to destroy the United States and pave the way for the rise of a global government and the Antichrist." He continues, "They will not stop until they have crippled the national economy, transforming the once-great United States into an impoverished nation with a severely weakened military and no influence on the world stage".

As a former financial advisor and founder of Frontier Research Publications, and host of *Bible Prophecy Revealed* on the Trinity Broadcast Network, Jeffrey goes on to say, "The reason the United States is not mentioned in Bible prophecy indicates it will not be a leading power in the world in end-time events." "By that time, he said, it will likely have collapsed and fallen into a state of near oblivion due to the national debt and the Federal Reserve's Bank staggering expansion of money supply."

If this was to happen and America faced an economic meltdown, it would probably survive, but the aftermath of such a collapse will affect America on the world stage where we would no longer be considered one of the most powerful nations in the world.

What can we do as consumers to protect our finances and investments? Most of the information I researched says the same thing. We should prepare to survive without government assistance, which unfortunately includes Social Security, Medicare, food stamps, Obamacare, and unemployment compensation. We need a plan for thriving or surviving on our own. Check with saving and/or investment banks to be certain your funds are safe by checking ratings with Weiss Ratings (weissratings.com). There are also suggestions by many articles to invest in gold or silver, which has always been a protection or hedge against the weakening dollar.

It would also be a safeguard to stock up on some extra food items such as dried or canned goods and have some containers of fresh drinking water available. Many people that I have talked to in my community suggest having extra batteries, a radio that runs on batteries, a portable generator for emergencies, candles, kerosene lamps, an alternate source of heat, and other crucial items that are applicable to each person's needs.

The hope is that we would be raptured before things got too terrible, but as God has said, we do not know the day or the hour, so it is best to be prepared in case of any emergency that may arise to protect our families. We can also prepare by praying to our Lord Jesus that this does not happen, yet as the seven year cycle shows us, the history of the Shemitah may repeat itself. America may be about to receive another warning of judgment from God for not following Him. Pray, pray and pray! Unfortunately, our political and financial methods of operating in the United States are on a downward spiral. Our political parties are usually at odds with each other and can't agree or disagree respectively. Our present federal government administration seems to be taking us down the road of "no return".

Our only hope is through national repentance and it is most likely too late for our whole nation to completely transform as a whole entity, but it is not too late for individuals to come to the Lord. It has been difficult for Christians to unite together and stand up for all the changes that have occurred in America, but it is time to do what we can and help as many people, who hopefully will listen, turn their lives over to Jesus to be saved and repent of their sins. He will forgive people for anything they have done in their lives, if they seriously want forgiveness, but you do need to ask and be genuinely remorseful.

If America continues on this path of self-destruction, we need to be prepared for what might happen. If a person does know what to do, then pray and ask God for guidance. In the Stillness, God, with His whispering voice, will nudge each person toward their own solution.

Many Christians are praying that the Lord will come soon for the Church in the way of the Rapture. What is the Rapture? The most glorious event yet to take place! Stay tuned....

CHAPTER 8

THE RAPTURE

For the Lord Himself will come down from heaven,
with a loud command,
with the voice of the archangel
and with the trumpet call of God,
and the dead in Christ will rise first.
After that, we who are still alive
and are left will be caught up together
with them in the clouds
to meet the Lord in the air.
And so, we will be with the Lord forever.
(1Thessalonians 4:15-17 NKJV)

<u>What is the Rapture?</u>

The Rapture is a "magnificent event", which God has promised to the Church. The promise is that someday, at the blowing of a trumpet and the shout of an archangel, Jesus will appear in the sky and take **UP** His Church, living and dead, to Heaven. The word "Church" are those people who believe in Jesus Christ, Son of God, with all their heart, mind and soul. They live their lives like they belong to Him. Jesus will return as a bridegroom for His bride, and that bride consists only of Church Age saints or believers.

This is the time, according to the New Testament, when Christ suddenly, "in the twinkling of an eye" will raise believers, first from the dead and then those who are still alive here on earth, up together in the clouds to meet the Lord in the air and be with him forever. The word "rapture" is a Latin word, the Greek term *harpazo*, which means "caught up" or "snatched up". The rapid "twinkling of an eye" is very sudden, very fast! In a quick blink of the eye, we could all be changed forever. The rapture is imminent, could happen at any moment, but no one knows the hour or the day, not even Jesus.

The rapture may be one of the most massive events of the Bible paralleling it to Noah's Ark and the flood. During the days of Noah's Ark, people ignored the warning that the earth would be flooded. In **Genesis 6:13**, God said to Noah, *"The end of all flesh has come before Me, for the earth is filled with violence through them; and behold, I will destroy them with the earth."*

In other words, as Ron Rhodes, author of *"The End Times in Chronological Order"* states, "the rapture is that glorious event in which the dead in Christ will be resurrected, living Christians will be instantly transformed into their resurrected bodies, and both groups will be caught up to meet Christ in the air and taken back to heaven. Yes, in an instant, living Christians will be with Christ in their immortal bodies. What a moment that will be!"

Are we ready for the Lord "Himself" to come down from heaven with a loud command, the voice of the archangel and the trumpet call of God? Most of us might answer, "I am not sure. What do I need to do to be ready?"

... Behold, I tell you a mystery: We shall not all sleep, but we shall all be changed –in a moment, in the twinkling of an eye, at the last trumpet. For the trumpet will sound, and the dead will be raised incorruptible, and we shall be changed. **(1 Corinthians 15:51-52)**

As scripture tells us, "Behold, I tell you a mystery. We will not all sleep, but we will all be changed in a moment." The Bible is giving us a warning to be ready for when the trumpet sounds; we will all be changed in the twinkling of an eye. At that precise moment you must be ready! God warns us to be ready, be watchful and be alert. If we are not ready, it will be too late and we will be *left behind*. Do we believe that the rapture could actually happen in our life time? Or are we asleep, perhaps *dead* asleep. Maybe our heads are in the sand, not wanting to know. Perhaps it is easier to say we don't believe rather than to do the work to find out the real truth. Here are a few questions to ask:

- Has someone in your life tried to encourage you to learn more about the Bible and Jesus, but you have brushed it aside?
- When you see a Christian show on TV, do you instantly change the channel?
- Are you from a family where you never or seldom attended church?
- Are you from a family that doesn't believe in God or a family that has a lukewarm relationship with God?

101

- Is your life busy with working, taking care of family and your home, running the kids to all their activities, watching mindless entertainment on TV, keeping up with Facebook, answering text messages, and all the other goings-on so there isn't enough room in your life to take time to read the Bible, take your family to church, and learn more about the love Jesus has for you?

If you answered "yes" to any of the above questions, you have ignored the call of Jesus. He calls for us to know Him by sending messages through friends, relatives, television, books, DVDs, cards, music, answered prayer, and most importantly, the *Holy Bible*, the only #1 bestselling book available for hundreds and hundreds of years. Jesus loves you and He is waiting!

Amazingly, the 7.3 billion people living in the World may not realize we are running out of time. Of the 7.3 billion people on earth, Christians make-up approximately 2.1 billion or 31% of the world according to www.worldometer.info. Of the 2.1 billion Christians in the World, it is estimated that only one-third or 700 million are what bible scholars classify as "real Christians".

Real Christians are people who dedicate their lives to Christ and follow His teachings and are not afraid to stand up for Christ. They want others to know the real love of Jesus and how He can change their lives if they trust in Him as their Savior. Then there are Christians who attend church on a superficial basis and may intellectually know stories of the Bible, but may not have Jesus in their hearts. The remaining group calls themselves Christians, but seldom attend church, open and study their bibles or attend bible studies. They are usually fearful of expressing their thoughts on Christianity for fear of persecution.

In **Revelation 3:16**, in the letter to the church of Laodiceans, *"So then, because you are lukewarm and neither cold nor hot, I will vomit you out of My mouth."* The Lord is clear He doesn't care for lukewarm Christians. He wants people to be passionate about Him.

It is reassuring that in our walk with Jesus that He has prepared a place for us in heaven and He will come back and take us to him. If we surrender our hearts to Jesus and not let our hearts be troubled, He will come back for us and take us with Him to be in His Father's house. Jesus goes on to comfort His Disciples in John 14:1-3:

"Do not let your hearts be troubled. Trust in God, trust also in me. In my Father's house are many rooms; if it were not so, I would have told you. I am going there to prepare a place for you. And if I go and prepare a place for you, I will come back and take you to be with me that you also may be where I am." **(John 14:1-3)**

Could this be the rapture? The Lord has prepared a place for us and He will come back and take us to be with Him. How exciting to know that we can Trust in God and His Son Jesus with all of our troubles. He loves us so much that He has prepared a place so that we may be there with Him in heaven.

WHEN WILL THE RAPTURE HAPPEN?

Questions are asked "when will the rapture happen"? Scripture is very clear that no one knows the day or the hour, not even the angels, nor the Son (Jesus) knows, but only the Father. Yet he tells us to be on guard, be alert and **WATCH! (Mark 13:36-37)** Do not let the Lord find you sleeping. This does not mean literally asleep, but "asleep" in knowing that the Lord gave His life for us, and we are saved by surrendering our lives to Him. Do you know the Lord, Jesus Christ? It is worth saying again that no human being knows the time of the rapture. God may give us signs & symbols that represent the end of times and that the rapture is imminent, but no one knows the day or the hour.

"Remember, No one knows about that day or hour, not even the angels in heaven, nor the Son, but only the Father. Be on guard! Be alert! You do not know when that time will come. He will come in the twinkling of an eye; do not let Him find you sleeping. What I say to you, I say to everyone: WATCH!"
(Mark 13:32-37)

"Now brothers, about times and dates we do not need to write to you for you know very well that the day of the Lord will come like a thief in the night. While people are saying "Peace" and "Safety", destruction will come on them suddenly, as labor pains on a pregnant woman and they will not escape." **(1 Thessalonians 5:1-3)**

According to author, Ron Rhodes, *The Popular Dictionary of Bible Prophecy*, "The New Testament teaches that the rapture is "imminent", which means "ready to take place" or "impending". There is nothing that must be prophetically fulfilled before the rapture occurs. The rapture is an event that can happen at any moment. Can you imagine the chaos alone by having approximately 700 million people vanish from the face of the earth to join the Lord?

The Bible offers many signs through scripture that the rapture will take place prior to the tribulation. In **Revelation 3:10**, Jesus promises the church in Philadelphia, *"I will keep you from the hour of trial that is coming on the whole world, to try those who dwell on the earth".* This scripture indicates that the church saints will not have to go through the seven years of tribulation. Church saints are people who belong, believe and follow Jesus *before* the rapture. Jesus promises the church that He will keep them from the hour of trial that is coming on the whole world.

Sadly, there will be many people fast asleep with their backs to the Lord. Oh, how my heart longs for them to be awakened, to be alert, and to be watchful, for the time is coming soon! How do we know for sure?

"But you, brothers & sisters, are not in darkness so that this day should surprise you like a thief. You are all sons of the light and sons of the day. We do not belong to the night or to the darkness. So then, let us not be like others, who are asleep, but let us be alert and self-controlled. Therefore, encourage one another and build each other up, just as you are doing." **(1 Thessalonians 5:4-11)**

I will repeat this many times throughout the book; it is clear through scripture that no one knows the exact time, day or hour the Lord will come, yet it does say to be *Watchful! Be on Guard! Be Alert!* If a friend told us that a thief would appear at our door at 2 am, wouldn't we want to be prepared? Would we not make extra preparations like putting extra locks on the doors, make a cell phone call to alert the police, ready our protection with a gun, knife or a bat, instruct our wife and children to stay at another place for the night and then "stand guard" all night? Of course, we would, yet, when we hear that the Lord is coming, people turn away and ignore it.

Our loving God is giving us the same warning that judgment and wrath will come upon the earth for those who do not believe. It clearly says in **1 Corinthians 16:22**: *"If anyone does not love the Lord—a curse be on him. Come, O Lord"!*

Most dialogue about the Rapture is about "when" is it appointed to happen, yet many biblical scholars of today seem to be strongly leaning on the pre-tribulation time frame. Other people position it at the mid-point of the Tribulation at the 3-1/2 year mark when the Antichrist makes his full appearance. Still others have suggested that it will occur at the end of the Tribulation, at the second coming of the Lord.

The Bible's word best infers that the Rapture will take place before the Tribulation. In Scripture we are told to **"watch"** or **"be ready"** for the appearance of our Lord.

*"Therefore you also **be ready**, for the Son of Man is coming at an hour you do not expect."* **(Matthew 24:44)**

"Watch *therefore, for you do not know what hour your Lord is coming."* **(Matthew 24:42)**

*"Blessed are those servants whom the master, when he comes, will find **watching."*** **(Luke 12:37)**

*"**Watch** therefore, and pray always that you may be counted worthy to escape all these things that will come to pass and to stand before the Son of Man".* **(Luke 21:36)**

The persistent warning throughout these scriptures is to be "watchful" and "to be ready" for our Lord could appear at any moment. The pre-Tribulation concept of the Rapture is the only one that allows for the "imminent" appearing of the Lord for His Church.

If you were to place the Rapture at the mid-point of the Tribulation, the imminent appearance of the Lord is nonexistent because other prophetic events must happen first like the Israeli peace treaty, the rebuilding of the Temple and the appearance of the Antichrist.

Another viewpoint in behalf of a pre-Tribulation Rapture comes to us in **Romans 5:9**, *"Much more then, having now been justified by his blood, we shall be saved from wrath through Him."* God promises to protect the Church from His wrath. The Book of Revelation points out that the wrath of God will be poured out during the entire period of the Tribulation; therefore, this is our best indicator that the rapture will happen sometime before the Tribulation. Here are three other scriptures that justify a pre-Tribulation Rapture.

"For God did not appoint us to wrath, but to obtain salvation through our Lord Jesus Christ." **(1 Thess 5:9)**

"To wait for His Son from heaven, whom He raised from the dead, even Jesus who delivers us from the wrath to come." **(1 Thessalonians 1:10)**

For the Lord Himself will come down from heaven,

with a loud command,
with the voice of the archangel
and with the trumpet call of God,
and the dead in Christ will rise first.
After that, we who are still alive
and are left will be caught up together
with them in the clouds
to meet the Lord in the air.
And so, we will be with the Lord forever.
(1Thessalonians 4:15-17 NKJV)

After studying scriptures, the one that stands out as the clearest and gives us the most vivid picture of the Rapture is **1 Thessalonians 4:15-17.**

In the Book of Revelation, it implies a pre-Tribulation Rapture with the first three chapters focusing on the letters to the seven churches. In **Revelation 4:1-2,** *"After these things I looked, and behold, a door standing open in heaven. And the first voice which I heard was like a trumpet speaking with me, saying, 'Come up here, and I will show you things which must take place after this.' Immediately, I was in the Spirit; and behold, a throne set in heaven, and One sat on the throne."* (Note the first voice that sounds like a trumpet.)

Ironically, the Church is not mentioned again until **Revelation 19:7-9**, when it is depicted as the "Bride of Christ"; for the marriage of the Lamb has come and His wife has made herself ready. In **versus 9**, He states, "Write: 'Blessed are those who are called to the marriage supper of the Lamb!'"

In **Revelation 19:11-16**, the door of Heaven opens again and Jesus (His Name is called the Word of God) rides in on a white horse. His armies of angels (the Church) in Heaven follow Him to strike the nations. On His thigh a name is written:

KING OF KINGS AND
LORD OF LORDS.

WHAT WILL THE RAPTURE LOOK LIKE TO THOSE LEFT BEHIND?

The world will be thrown into instant chaos! Can you imagine millions of people from earth just disappearing in an instant? What a rude awakening to billions of people to find out they have been left behind. Their loved ones, their children, their friends and family have just disappeared. Can you imagine in America alone, planes, flying through the air, would have a pilot or copilot disappear leaving the plane to crash or air traffic controllers would disappear leaving planes on their own to land or take off? Believers will vanish from their cars causing wrecks throughout the entire highway system and doctors and/or patients will disappear from surgery rooms.

One of the biggest shocks will be people who believed they were Christian; only to find out they didn't have Jesus in their hearts, but only in their intellect with book knowledge. Unbelieving husbands will be frantically looking for their believing wives and non-Christian wives searching for their Christian husbands. The saddest moments will be when the children vanish from homes, schools, daycares, and playgrounds, while frantic parents desperately search for them. The heartbreak will be unbearable!

It is almost impossible to imagine how chaotic it might be in our world. There will be those unbelievers who are skeptical and not able to comprehend that the rapture just took place. I imagine many reporters and news analysts will attempt to make desperate sense out of millions of people evaporating into the cloudy atmosphere. Once the world realizes that Christian believers are the common thread of all who vanished, then the stark awareness of realism will begin to unfold. Those people left behind have the unfathomable chore of dealing with the aftermath and reevaluating their own belief systems. Some may realize immediately what has happened and fall to their knees and instantaneously call on the Lord, "Oh God, please save me, I didn't think you were real!"

...For we will all stand before God's judgment seat. It is written: "As surely as I live," says the Lord, "every knee will bow before Me; Every tongue will confess to God." **(Romans 14:10-11)**

"That at the name of Jesus every knee should bow, in heaven and on earth and under the earth, and every tongue confess that Jesus Christ is Lord, to the glory of God the Father." **(Philippians 2:10-11)**

"I am the Lord, and there is no other; apart from Me there is no God. I will strengthen you, though you have not acknowledged Me, so that from the rising of the sun to the place of its setting men may know there is none besides Me. I am the Lord and there is no other." **(Isaiah 45:5-6)**

Wake up! The time is near! So then, let us not be like others, who are asleep, but let us be alert and self-controlled. There are millions if not billions of people in the world who do not know Jesus. They are unfortunately ASLEEP and will not be raptured. There will be a massive group of people in the world left behind to face seven years of the great tribulation.

Anyone standing by the graveside of a departed loved one or friend considers the questions that arise: What do I believe about this event called death? Even knowledgeable Christians have to defend themselves against waves of sadness and longing by remembering the promises of Jesus Christ concerning faith and eternal life. Those promises— promises based on the Resurrection—give the Christian renewed hope that is sometimes clouded by grief.

It is important to know that even though it can be frightening, the events happening in our world have to happen. **Matthew 24:6** states it clearly. *"When you hear of wars or rumors of wars, but see to it that you are not alarmed. Such things must happen, but the end is still to come."* If you are close to God, He will protect you, He will rapture you up with Him in the Clouds and you will avoid all of the Tribulation.

There is symbolism found in the Jewish wedding traditions that also confirms a pre-tribulation Rapture. After the engagement, the groom returns to his father's house to prepare a wedding chamber for his bride. He would return for his bride at an unexpected moment, so the bride was constantly ready for his arrival. When the groom returned, he took his bride back to his father's house to the chamber he had prepared. He and his bride were remained in the chamber for seven days. When they emerged, a great wedding feast would be celebrated.

Similarly, Jesus has returned to Heaven to prepare a place for His bride (His believers), the Church. When He returns for His bride, He will take her to His Father's heavenly home. There He will remain with His bride for seven years (The Tribulation period). The period will end with "the marriage supper of the Lamb" described in **Revelation 19:9**. The seven days in the wedding chamber symbolize the seven years that Jesus and His bride (the church) remain in Heaven during the Tribulation.

In summary, these passages and symbolisms teach us that the shout of an archangel and the blowing of a trumpet will announce the sudden appearance of Jesus in the Heavens. **(1 Thessalonians 4:13-18)** The dead in Christ will be resurrected and rise up to meet the Lord in the clouds. Then the ones still alive and are left here on earth will be caught up together to join the dead in the clouds to meet the Lord in the air. And so, will remain with the Lord forever. Absolutely, the Rapture is a comforting thought if you are a true believer and follower of Jesus Christ. It encourages Christians to be pure in heart knowing the time is near! Those believers who are living when the Rapture happens will not even experience death. They will be gathered up to join the Lord in the Air! Wow! Could we be that generation of believers that Jesus said "would not die"?

If you are not a Christian, your only hope is to reach out in faith and receive the free gift of God's salvation which He has provided through His Son, Jesus. **(John 3:16)** Please don't waste another minute, for the Rapture could happen at any time. Your Lord is waiting for you!

The Lord's coming is mentioned over 532 times in the Bible and one of the few subjects in the Bible that is repeated so many times. I believe the Lord wants to give us every chance in the world to believe in Him. He wants to save us for He is our savior, who gave His own life for us. If each of us were to count how many times people in our lives have tried to teach us about the Bible, invited us to church, invited us to a bible study, given us a Christian book, or talked to us about Jesus, we would realize that we have had many chances to learn about Christ, yet maybe we turned way. We have turned away from the One who loves us the most.

Just like an earthly father, who also loves his children, he may need to discipline them about the consequences of life and at times practice tough love to help the child understand that what he is doing wrong will hurt him. Many children or teenagers will turn away, not wanting to be told what to do and they will continue on the path of destruction. Without discipline, they will be led astray. Just like an earthly father, our heavenly father gives us many chances to come to him, but if we continue to rebel, He will eventually have to discipline us or offer his wrath of judgment and we too will suffer the consequences. Unfortunately, we will eventually be judged for turning away from the Lord and then be left behind to face the great tribulation. I personally can't imagine the sinking feeling people will have as they realize the rapture was 'real' and they didn't take it seriously.

If by chance you are reading this book after the rapture and find yourself *left behind*, you will have another chance to come to know the Lord, but the period of "grace" will have expired. This means, through Paul's writing in the New Testament, God the Holy Spirit withdraws from restraining evil within the minds of people who are left behind. Therefore, there shall be more violence, immorality, and chaos within the regime of the Antichrist as he enters the world to lead those left behind.

Those who have rejected Christ will fall prey to the temptation and enticement of evil the Antichrist offers. If a person can be true to the Lord during this time, not take the mark of the beast (666) and be willing to suffer as a martyr for Christ through the Great Tribulation, he will be saved and spend eternity with the Lord, our God. These people will be called the Tribulation Saints. Unfortunately, they will have to go through the seven years of tribulation, a period described in **Matthew 24:21** as *"such severity that no period in history past or future will equal it"*. The chapter on the "Tribulation" will show us that we definitely want to avoid the events of this seven year period.

> **Look for the blessed hope and glorious appearing of our great God and Savior Jesus Christ.**
>
> **Titus 2:13**

> **And if I go and prepare a place for you, I will come again and receive you to Myself; that where I am, *there* you may be also.**
>
> **John 14:1**

Seven years of TRIBULATION

CHAPTER 9

What is the Tribulation?

According to Revelation, this will be a unique and especially *intense* period of trouble that will come sometime after the rapture of the Church. Unfortunately, those left behind will have to go through the dreadful seven-year tribulation period. Jesus taught his disciples that they should expect difficulties and troubles in this world.

"These things I have spoken to you, that in Me you may have peace. In the world you will have tribulation; but be of good cheer, I have overcome the world."

(John 16:33)

After the shock of the rapture, countless people will flock to the church to get closer to the Lord. The churches will be overrun with people wanting and yearning to know more of the Bible. After all, they had just witnessed the power of God's hand rapturing up to the heavens all of His Christian followers. They now have little doubt that there is a God, but may not be sure what to do next. The chaos after the Rapture will truly be a time of readjustment into a whole different world and may take years to retain some sense of

115

normality. As people flock to the church to find out more about the truth of Jesus Christ, the Book of Revelation reveals a world turning upside down as the Lamb of God opens up the seals to reveal judgments upon the earth.

Note*: As an author, I will provide a brief outline of tribulation events, but in order to understand the pertinent details, I recommend reading the Book of Revelations and then joining a Bible Study or buying a study guide to help interpret tribulation events.*

The Seven Seals – Only the Lamb of God opens the seals. The first four seals are judgments upon the earth and the last 3 seals paint an even more threatening picture of God interceding in the affairs of people on earth. The last three judgments are harsher than the first four seals.

First Seal: The Conqueror comes on a white horse. He has a bow and a crown, which was given to him, and he went out to conquer. **(Revelation 6:1-2)**

Second Seal: This person who comes on a fiery red horse, with a great sword, is granted the ability to take peace from the earth, and that people shall kill one another resulting in conflict on earth. **(Revelation 6:3-4)** Pre-rapture, we are aware of conflicts; especially in the Middle East, where there are many struggles and battles. During the opening of the second seal, this will increase beyond our ability to comprehend and may spread throughout the whole world.

Third Seal: A black horse and he who sat on it had a pair of scales in his hand. Black usually is associated with famine in the Bible. In the early days of the tribulation, food will be in short supply, and people will have to work all day just to get enough food to eat. The luxuries of the rich such as wine and oil will remain unused. **(Revelation 6:5-6)** It is recorded that a man will have to work all day just to get enough money for his daily food. With a shortage of food, every man will be out for himself to survive.

<u>Fourth Seal</u>: A pale horse comes and he who sat on it was Death, and Hades followed with him. Power was given to them, over a fourth of the earth, to kill with a sword, with hunger, with death, all the beasts of the earth resulting in widespread death on earth. **(Revelation 6:7-8)** It is hard to comprehend, yet there will be great stress and chaos as more death prevails over 25% of the earth.

<u>Fifth Seal</u>: Under the altar, the souls of those who had been slain for the word of God said, *"How long, O Lord, holy and true, until You judge and avenge our blood on those who dwell on the earth?"* They were given a white robe and told to rest a little longer, until both the number of their fellow servants and their brethren, who would be killed as they were, was completed. This is commonly called "The Cry of the Martyrs". **(Revelation 9-11)**

Martyrs are Christians who give their lives for Jesus. This may include Christians who were beheaded, killed for standing up for Jesus or just by the very nature of being Christian. Fox News reports on 6/2/13 that "a staggering 100,000 Christians are killed annually because of their faith and several human rights groups claim such anti-Christian violence is on the rise in countries such as Pakistan, Nigeria, Libya, and Egypt." The Lord has these souls with Him in Heaven and He will avenge those who committed such barbaric acts. During this 5th seal, the Lord gives the Martyrs a white robe and asks them to rest a little longer.

<u>Sixth Seal</u>: When the sixth seal was opened there was a great earthquake; and the sun became black and the moon became like blood. The stars of heaven fell to the earth. Then the sky receded as a scroll when it is rolled up, and every mountain and island was moved out of its place. All the men of the earth, from kings to slaves, hid themselves in the caves and in the rocks of the mountains. They said, *"Fall on us and hide us from the face of Him who sits on the throne and from the wrath of the Lamb! For the great day of His wrath has come, and who is able to stand?"* **(Revelation 6:12-17)**

Throughout the Old Testament, earthquakes are used to symbolize the *"shaking of the earth with the final judgment of the Lord"*. **(Joel 2:10)** Jesus prophesies that the event described in **Revelation 6:12-17**, will precede the Day of the Lord. Prophets declare that mid-day darkness would again fall over the earth at the beginning of the Tribulation. **(Joel 2:30)**

<u>Seventh Seal</u>: The unique seventh seal is the introduction to the seven trumpets. **Revelation 8:1** says, *"When He opened the seventh seal, there was silence in heaven for about half an hour."* Can you imagine thirty minutes of "silence"? Doesn't it make you wonder why? This is truly the silence before the "storm". Seven angels, who stood before God, were given seven trumpets. Then another angel, having a golden censer, came and stood at the altar. He was given incense that he should offer it with the prayers of all the saints upon the golden altar which was before the throne. And the smoke of the incense, with the prayers of the saints, ascended before God from the angel's hand. Then the angel filled it with fire and threw it to the earth.

There were noises, thundering, lightning, and an earthquake. The seven angels then prepared themselves to sound. **(Revelation 8:1-6)**

As you can see from each seal, the events progressively get worse as they are opened up. God is unhappy that we have forsaken Him. His wrath will judge the unbelieving world. The seven trumpets come next and the results are even more staggering!

Seven Trumpets

First Trumpet *"The first angel sounded: And hail and fire followed, mingled with blood, and they were thrown to the earth. And a third of the trees were burned up, and all green grass was burned up."* **(Revelation 8:7)** To have one third of the trees burning up and all the green grass burning is a monster of a fire.

Second Trumpet *"Then the second angel sounded: And something like a great mountain burning with fire was thrown into the sea and a third of the sea became blood. And a third of the living creatures in the sea died, and a third of the ships were destroyed."* **(Revelation 8:8)** This sounds similar to a huge volcano or many volcanoes being thrown into the sea where it turns to blood and one-third of the sea life dies and ships are destroyed. Since oceans cover about 75% of the earth surface, the results of this will be staggering and unconceivable.

Third Trumpet *"Then the third angel sounded: And a great star fell from heaven, burning like a torch and it fell on a third of the rivers and on the springs of water. The name of the star is Wormwood. A third of the waters became* *wormwood and many men died from the water, because it was made bitter." **(Relevation 8:10-11)*** Being in human form, we try to figure out what this might be that we are familiar with...comet or a meteorite. Wormwood is a plant with a very bitter taste. In the Bible it symbolizes the bitterness that comes from sorrow and calamity. **(Jeremiah 9:15)** Having this star fall on one third of the rivers and springs will affect the quality of drinking water causing many hardships and people to die.

Fourth Trumpet *"Then the fourth angel sounded: And a third of the sun was struck, a third of the moon, and a third of the stars, so that a third of them were darkened. A third of the day did not shine, and likewise the night. And I looked, and I heard an angel flying through the midst of heaven saying with a loud voice, "Woe, woe, woe to the inhabitants of the earth, because of the remaining blasts of the trumpet of the three angels who are about to sound!"*

(Revelation 8:12-13)

"Woe, woe, woe" in scripture is a heart stopper! The angel is shouting these words to the people left on earth. Can they survive? It is bad enough to have one third of the green vegetation on fire; one third of the sea turned to blood and sea life destroyed; one third of the rivers and springs unusable for drinking, and one third of our beautiful sun, moon and stars darkened. It is about to get worse.

Fifth Trumpet *"Then the fifth angel sounded: And I saw a star fallen from heaven to the earth. To him was given the key to the bottomless pit. And he opened the bottomless pit, and smoke arose out of the pit like the smoke of a great furnace. So the sun and the air were darkened because of the smoke of the pit. Then out of the smoke locusts came upon the earth. And to them was given power, as the scorpions of the earth have power. They were commanded not to harm the grass of the earth, or any green thing, or any tree, but only those men who do not have the seal of God on their foreheads. And they were not given authority to kill them, but to torment them for five months. Their torment was like the torment of a scorpion when it strikes a man. In those days men will seek death and will not find it; they will desire to die, and death will flee from them."*

(Revelation 9:1-6)

This feels like a very dark, hellish place with the sun darkened, smoke from the bottomless pit and five months of torment from the locust when you really want to die but death escapes you. This is severe punishment for those who arrogantly rebelled against God. If we were tormented for five months, we would become like demons, unable to cope or survive. It seems so much easier to be humble and love God with all of our hearts and avoid this hell. I personally once had a sign on my bulletin board that said, "If you are going through Hell, don't Stop." Keep moving forward trusting in God to take you through.

*"One **woe** is past. Behold, still two more **woes** are coming after these things."* **(Revelation 9:12)**

<u>Sixth Trumpet</u> *"Then the sixth angel sounded: And I heard a voice from the four horns of the golden altar which is before God, saying to the sixth angel who had the trumpet, "Release the four angels who are bound at the great river Euphrates". So the four angels, who had been prepared for the hour and day and month and year, were released to kill a third of mankind. Now the number of the army of the*

121

*horsemen was two hundred million; I heard the number of them. And thus I saw the horses in the vision: those who sat on them had breastplates of fiery red, hyacinth blue, and sulfur yellow; and the heads of the horses were like the heads of lions; and out of their mouths came fire, smoke, and brimstone. By these three plagues a third of mankind was killed—by the fire and the smoke and the brimstone which came out of their mouths." **(Revelation 13-18)**

This sixth trumpet is the answer to prayer for the tribulation martyrs. The golden altar is where the martyrs' souls resided awaiting avenge for those who had persecuted and killed them. Remember in **Revelation 6:9-11**, the Fifth Seal, the martyrs from under the altar asked God, *"when will it be time and God says to wait a little while longer."* The four angels are instructed to kill one third of mankind. The number of the army will be 200,000,000. What horrible bloodshed is yet to transpire!

"I saw still another mighty angel coming down from heaven, clothed with a cloud. And a rainbow was on his head; his face was like the sun, and his feet like pillars of fire. He had a little book open in his hand. And he set his right foot on the sea and his left foot on the land, and cried with a loud voice, as when a lion roars. When he cried out, seven thunders uttered their voices. Now when the seven thunders uttered their voices, I was about to write; but I heard a voice from heaven saying to me, "Seal up the things which the seven thunders uttered, and do not write them." **(Revelation 10:1-4)**

"Then the voice which I heard from heaven spoke to me again and said, "Go, take the little book which is open in the hand of the angel who stands on the sea and on the

earth." *So, I went to the angel and said to him, "Give me the little book." And he said to me, "Take and eat it; and it will make your stomach bitter, but it will be as sweet as honey in your mouth."* **(Revelation 10:8-9)** *"You must prophesy again about many peoples, nations, tongues, and kings."* **(Revelation 10:10)**

This judgement represents that John, who heard the angels speak to him, would feel joy (honey) in proclaiming God's word, but sorrow (bitterness) in realizing its rejection by those who would not hear. Preaching prophetic truth is a bittersweet experience.

You will notice that the 7th trumpet has not sounded yet. It was sealed up and John did not write it. There is a pause between the 6th and 7th trumpet for a period of grace. This pause offers us mercy, love and encouragement from God. First He sends an angel to hear; secondly, we have the two witnesses and thirdly, we have the twenty-four elders in heaven.

TWO WITNESSES

In **Revelation 11:1-14**, the two witnesses are considered to be real human beings, possibly Elijah and Moses. They are called olive trees and lampstands to suggest their ministry of light in the mystery of the Holy Spirit. The temple of God is measured or judged against those who are worshiping there. The temple will be rebuilt by Jews who have been gathered in Israel sometime during the tribulation period. The witnesses will have power to prophesy 1,260 days clothed in sackcloth. *"They will have the power to shut heaven, so that no rain falls in the days of their prophecy; and they will have power over waters to turn* *them to blood, and to strike the earth with all plagues, as often as they desire."* **(Revelation 11:6)**

When they finish their testimony the beast (antichrist) will come out of the bottomless pit and make war against them and kill them. The two witnesses' dead bodies will lie in the streets three and one-half days. People rejoiced and were merry to see them dead on the street, for these two prophets had tormented them with their testimony. After three and one-half days, the breath of God entered the two dead bodies and they stood on their feet and great fear fell on those who had rejoiced. The two witnesses ascended into heaven and their enemies saw them go. In the same hour there was a great earthquake and one tenth of the city fell and 7,000 people were killed. The rest of the people were afraid and gave glory to the God of Heaven.

*"The second **woe** is past. Behold, the third **woe** is coming quickly."* **(Revelation 11:14)**

<u>Seventh Trumpet</u>   *"Then the seventh angel sounded: And there were loud voices in heaven, saying, 'The kingdoms of this world have become the kingdoms of our Lord and of His Christ, and he shall reign forever and ever!' And the twenty-four elders who sat before God on their thrones fell on their faces and worshiped God, saying:*
"We give You thanks, O Lord God Almighty,
The One who is and who was and who is to come,
Because You have taken Your great power and
*   reigned.*
The nations were angry and Your wrath has come,
And the time of the dead, that they should be judged,
And that You should reward Your servants the
*   prophets and the saints,*

And those who fear Your name, small and great,
And should destroy those who destroy the earth."

"Then the temple of God was opened in heaven and the ark of His covenant was seen in His temple. And there was lightning, noises, thundering's, an earthquake, and great hail." **(Revelation 11:15-19)**

WOE...in heaven the transition of power to Jesus Christ as King of Kings and Lord of Lords has sounded! The kingdoms on earth are still under Satan's authority, but God has control over what is happening and what is about to happen. We are about to have the final conflict in heaven between God and Satan, all their armies of angels and the humans who carry out the battles on earth.

The Woman, the Child, and the Dragon

"Now a great sign appeared in heaven: a woman clothed with the sun, with the moon under her feet, and on her head a garland of twelve stars. Then being with child, she cried out in labor and in pain to give birth." **(Revelation 12:1-2)** The woman represents Israel trying to give birth to a child—our Lord Jesus Christ.

"And another sign appeared in heaven: behold, a great, fiery red dragon (Satan) having seven heads and ten horns, and seven diadems on his heads. His tail drew a third of the stars of heaven and threw them to the earth. And the dragon stood before the woman who was ready to give birth, to devour her Child as soon as it was born. She bore a male Child who was to rule all nations with a rod of iron. And her Child was caught up to God and His throne. Then the woman fled into the wilderness, where she has a place

125

prepared by God that they should feed her there one thousand two hundred and sixty days." (1,260 days)
(Relevation12:3-6)

Satan here is described as having seven heads, the number symbolizing completeness in the Bible. The seven heads convey power and his universal power and evil spirit. Satan's goal throughout the Bible has always been to destroy Christ, so here it shows him ready to devour the child when the woman gives birth. God has more power than Satan and catches the male Child, Jesus, up to His throne, which depicts the resurrection. The woman, (Israel) is then in the wilderness, protected by God for 1,260 days.

Satan Thrown Out of Heaven

The battle continues between God and Satan as a war breaks out in Heaven. Michael and his angels fought with the dragon (Satan); and the dragon and his angels fought, but they did not prevail, nor was a place found for them in heaven any longer. So the great dragon was cast out, that serpent of old, called the Devil and Satan, who deceives the whole world; he was cast to the earth, and his angels were cast out with him.   **(Revelation 12:7-9)**

In **Revelation 13**, The Antichrist appears on the scene as the Beast from the Sea at approximately the mid-point of 3-1/2 years of the Tribulation. The Antichrist rules and unleashes persecution on all believers. The Antichrist is a lawless man who will come in Satan's power, demanding to be worshipped as God, destroying all those who love God.

According to **Daniel 8:23-25**, the characteristics of the Antichrist are dramatic in appearance, destined to do evil, dynamic in leadership, demonic in power, destructive in his reign, deceitful in his practice, and disguises his cruelty with peace promises. He will be charming, persuasive and popular beyond measure. The world will not know him as the "Antichrist," but by some attractive name and appealing title. But just as the word "Antichrist" suggests, he will be the opposite of the Lord Jesus Christ in every way. He is given great authority to continue to rule for 42 months (3-1/2 years to the end of the Tribulation period).

All who dwell on earth will want to worship him. Jesus tells us that, shortly before His return, the Antichrist will arise during a time of global chaos and confusion, when the world is in political, social, financial and ecological upheaval. The terrified people of the world, desperate for a strong leader, will turn to this man and give him control of the governments of the world.   Daniel tells us that the Antichrist will speak *"boastfully"* **(Dan. 7:8)**, yet it is clear that these will not be empty boasts. The Antichrist will appear to possess superhuman brilliance. He'll be the ultimate smooth talker, the greatest con man who ever lived, and he'll unite the nations under his rule. At first, he'll seem to be a wise and benevolent dictator, bringing peace, prosperity and hope. But once he is firmly in control of the gears and levers of power, he'll reveal his true intentions.

Another Beast from the Earth, the False Prophet, also joins the Antichrist and exercises all the same authority as the Antichrist. He performs great signs to deceive and causes all people, both small and great, rich and poor, to receive a mark on their right hand or on their forehead. No one may buy or sell except one who has the mark of the beast or his number 666.

In **Revelation 14**, as the Antichrist rules, a Lamb standing on Mount Zion presents 144,000 men who are spiritual virgins and redeemed Jews from earth. They are the ones who follow the Lamb wherever He goes. They are without fault before the throne of God. They are protected by God as they stand tall and preach to this generation of people through the tribulation.

The proclamations of three angels preach the everlasting gospel to those who dwell on earth, and warning people not to worship the antichrist nor receive the mark of 666. For those who do will be tormented with fire and brimstone forever and ever. For those who do not receive the mark or worship the Antichrist and keep the commandments of God and the faith of Jesus, *"Blessed are the dead who die in the Lord from now on."* **(Rev 14:13)**

Revelation 15-17 reveals the worst of the worst; the seven angels with the seven last plagues. God's final wrath is complete with these seven bowls. The bowls are described briefly here as:

First Bowl: Loathsome Sores for men who had received the mark of the beast or worshiped him.

Second Bowl: The Sea turns to Blood as every living creature in the sea dies.

Third Bowl: The Waters turn to Blood as the rivers and springs of water turn to blood.

Fourth Bowl: Men are scorched by the sun with great heat and fire.

Fifth Bowl: Darkness and Pain as the last bowl is poured out on the throne of the Antichrist and his kingdom and they gnawed their tongues in pain.

Sixth Bowl: Euphrates River dries up so the way of the kings from the east might be prepared and the whole world, as they gather for the battle of Armageddon, the great day of God Almighty.

"Alleluia! For the Lord God Omnipotent reigns! Let us be glad and rejoice and give Him glory, for the marriage of the Lamb has come, and His wife has made herself ready." "Blessed are those who are called to the marriage supper of the Lamb!"   **(Revelation 19:6, 9)**

Revelation 19:19-20 states that the Antichrist and the false prophet were destroyed supernaturally and cast alive into the lake of fire burning with brimstone.

Revelation 20 reveals that Satan is then bound for a thousand years and cast into a bottomless pit and a seal is set upon him so that he will not deceive the nations any more until the thousand years are finished. He will then be released for a short while.

This leads us to the wonderful time of saints and believers reigning with Christ for a peaceful 1000 years or millennium. The souls of those who had been beheaded for their witness to Jesus and the Word of God, and the people who did not worship the beast nor receive the 666 mark of the beast, ALL live and reign with Christ for 1000 years. Just think that when Christ comes back to reign during the Millennium, every believer's youthful resurrected body, from Adam onward, will be there to live peacefully with Him. This is called the first resurrection. The rest of the dead, the unsaved through the ages, will be raised after the Millennium is finished to stand before the Great White Throne of Judgment.

Remember, if by chance you are reading this book after the rapture and find yourself *left behind*, you will have another chance to come to know the Lord, but the period of "grace" will have expired.   God the Holy Spirit withdraws from restraining evil within the minds of people who are left behind.   Therefore, there shall be more violence, immorality, and chaos within the regime of the Antichrist as he enters the world to lead those left behind.   If a person can be true to the Lord during this time and suffer through the events of the Tribulation or be martyred for the Lord, he will be saved and spend eternity with the Lord, our God. Unfortunately, they will have to go through the seven years of tribulation, a period described in Matthew 24:21 as *"such severity that no period in history past or future will equal it"*.

It is important to remember if you are left behind to keep your eyes on the Lord and worship only Jesus Christ with all your heart, mind and soul.   Do not worship the Antichrist or take the mark of the beast, 666 or succumb to the pressures of the world and you will be saved and spend eternity with our Lord. The False Prophet will try to get you to take the mark of the Beast of 666 to allure you with the promise of being able to buy or sell food, water and other essentials.   But, it will be better to starve to death than take the mark of the Beast where you would spend eternity in a continual hell of fire and brimstone. Many Christians during the Tribulation will be martyred and die for their faith. Your promise is that Jesus will reward you with eternity in heaven with Him forever and ever.

> **Be always on the watch and pray that you may be able to escape all that is about to happen, and that you may be able to stand before the Son of Man.**
> **Luke 21:36**

CHAPTER 10

The SECOND COMING OF CHRIST

Did you know that "the second coming of Christ" is mentioned 318 times in the New Testament? Dr. David Jeremiah, states in his book, *What in the World is Going On?* that "scholars count 1845 biblical references to the Second Coming, including 318 in the New Testament. The Lord Himself referred to His return twenty-one times. The Second Coming is second only to faith as the most dominant subject in the New Testament." The second coming of Christ is also referred to as "The Day of the Lord" or the "Son of Man".

In Jesus' first coming, He came as a baby born in a manger, wrapped in swaddling clothes. He was surrounded by hay, by animals and common people such as Joseph and Virgin Mary. His voice was the small cry of a baby and He was the Lamb of God who came to bring salvation. In His second coming, He will roar in as a lion, to judge the world.

131

If you believe in Genesis 1:1 **"In the beginning God created the heavens and the earth"**, then the truth remains that in the Bible, God's Word, clearly tells us that Christ will return for a second time. It tells us 318 times. Before He comes a second time, there will be a rapture of the church of true Christians, followed by a seven year Tribulation period of great turmoil. It is well-defined in the Word of the Bible that the Lord is coming and we all need to be ready! Here are a few scriptures that speak to the "Son of Man" returning:

"Therefore keep watch, because you do not know on what day your Lord will come. But understand this: If the owner of the house had known at what time of night the thief was coming, he would have kept watch and would not have let his house be broken into. So you also must be ready, because the Son of Man will come at an hour when you do not expect him." **(Matthew 24:42-44)**

"...This same Jesus, who was taken up from you into heaven, will so come in like manner as you saw Him go into heaven." **(Acts 1:11)**

"Behold, the day of the Lord is coming, and your spoil will be divided in your midst." **(Zechariah 14:1)**

"Then the LORD will go forth and fight against those nations, As He fights in the day of battle. ⁴ And in that day His feet will stand on the Mount of Olives, which faces Jerusalem on the east. And the Mount of Olives shall be split in two, from east to west, making a very large valley; half of the mountain shall move toward the north and half of it toward the south." **(Zechariah 14:3-4)**

Upon reading **Zechariah 14:1-9**, a prophet who wrote this 500 years before the arrival of Jesus, we catch a truthful glimpse into the future that *"Behold the Lord is Coming"--* *" The Lord will go forth and fight against those nations, as He fights in the day of battle. And in that day His feet will stand on the Mount of Olives, which faces Jerusalem on the east".* The Lord even tells us where his feet will stand on the Mount of Olives when he returns.

And, then the Lord goes on to say what will happen next. *"The Mount of Olives shall be split in two, from east to west, making a very large valley. Yes, you shall flee. It shall come to pass that there is no light. The lights will diminish. It shall be one day which is known to the Lord— neither day nor night. But at evening time it shall happen that it will be light. It shall come to pass in that day that there will be no light; And in that day it shall be that living waters shall flow from Jerusalem, Half of them toward the eastern sea and half of them toward the western sea; In both summer and winter it shall occur."*

"And the LORD *shall be King over all the earth. In that day it shall be, 'The* LORD *is one,' and His name one."*
(Zechariah 14:1-9)

In the New Testament, approximately 560 years later, Jesus Himself speaks through Matthew about His second coming.

"For as the lightning comes from the east and flashes to the west, so also will the coming of the Son of Man be. Immediately after the tribulation of those days the sun will be darkened, and the moon will not give its light; the stars will fall from heaven and the powers of the heavens will be

shaken. Then the sign of the Son of Man will appear in heaven and then all the tribes of the earth will mourn, and they will see the Son of Man coming on the clouds of heaven with power and great glory." **(Matthew 24:27, 29-30)**

"And He will send His angels with a great sound of a trumpet, and they will gather together His elect from the four winds, from one end of heaven to the other." (Matthew 24:31)

"Assuredly, I say to you, this generation will by no means pass away till all these things take place. Heaven and earth will pass away, but My words will by no means pass away." **(Matthew 24:34-35)**

"But of that day and hour no one knows, not even the angels of heaven, but My Father only. But as the days of Noah were, so also will the coming of the Son of Man be. For as in the days before the flood, they were eating, and drinking, marrying and giving in marriage, until the day that Noah entered the ark, And did not know until the flood came and took them all away, also will the coming of the Son of Man be." **(Matthew 24:36-39)**

In the last Book of the Bible, there are two scriptures: one in **Revelation 1:7-8** and the other in **Revelation 22**: that boldly state:

"Behold, He is coming with clouds, and every eye will see Him, even they who pierced Him. And all the tribes of the earth will mourn because of Him. Even so, Amen. I am the Alpha and the Omega, the Beginning and the End," says the Lord, "who is and who was and who is to come, the Almighty." **(Revelation 1:7-8)**

"Behold, I am coming quickly! Blessed is he who keeps the words of the prophecy of this book
(Revelation 22:7)

Our King will return, after the seven years of tribulation, to rule over the nations, to reign over the people, to judge the earth, rescue the righteous from the wicked, throw the wicked into the Lake of Fire, and appoint his kingdom. He will be royally clothed in a robe dipped in blood accompanied by His army of angels, the heavens will be open, the last trumpet will sound and His voice will thunder like the sound of many waters. The Lord's army-of-angels is the group of people who were raptured as the Church. They will reign with the Lord forever.

In His second coming, He will not be the Lamb, but the **Lion** who brings judgment. Remember, Jesus' birth was prophesized in the Old Testament to happen. The Lord's second coming has been prophesized and we are aware of the signs of the end times and told to be WATCHFUL, BE ALERT, BE READY, for no one knows the day or the hour, not even the angels, nor Jesus himself...only His Father, God!

Scripture tells us a story. Scripture gives us a message. Scripture gives us a WARNING to be WATCHFUL for the Son of Man will come in His glory, with all the holy angels, and sit on the throne of His glory. All the nations will be gathered before Him and He will separate them one from another. We will all be judged!

Yet, scripture also gives us the message that God desires us to know about Christ's return. It is no accident that the second coming of Christ is mentioned 318 times in the New Testament. He does not want us to ignore this important detail. He wants us to know so we can be

135

prepared. God's deep desire is to have everyone know Him intimately and believe in Him with all their heart.

The Pharisees gathered around Jesus and asked, *"Teacher, which is the greatest commandment in the Law?" Jesus replied: "Love the Lord your God with all your heart and with all your soul and all your mind. This is the first and greatest commandment. And the second is like it: 'Love your neighbor as yourself.'"* All the Law and the Prophets hang on to these two commandments."

(Matthew 22:36-40)

According to Fern Flaming, instructor for Women's Ministry at Ranch Chapel, "Proverbs 1-3 provides us with life lessons on being wise or being a fool. Fools reject discipline, reject God's commandments, tempt others to sin, are ignorant, and engage in acts that are dishonoring and result in anger, bitterness and possibly incarceration".

"A wise man will hear and increase knowledge and a man of understanding will attain wise counsel"..."The fear of the Lord is the beginning of knowledge, BUT fools despise wisdom and instruction." **(Proverbs 1:4-5, 7-8)**

In **Proverbs 6:16-19**: *"There are six things the Lord hates, a proud look, a lying tongue, hands that shed innocent blood, a heart that devises wicked plans, feet that are swift in running to evil, a false witness who speaks lies, and one who creates conflict among his brothers."* **Proverbs 2:1-5:** *"My son, if you receive my words, and treasure my commands within you so that you give your ear to wisdom and apply your heart to understanding, then you will understand the fear of the Lord and find the knowledge of God."*

Be wise, follow God, believe in God, and obey God and you shall enter the Kingdom of God. A foolish man will be self-destructive without the knowledge and understanding of

God. **Proverbs 1:28-29** says it clearly as the Lord speaks, *"Then (the fools) they will call on me, but I will not answer; they will seek me diligently, but they will not find me. Because they hated knowledge and did not choose the fear of the Lord."* Remember that the God who gives His warnings and judgments is also the same God who heals and restores. When we "fear" the Lord, we honor and respect Him for He is God Almighty, the God of the Universe. He gives us wisdom, shields us from evil, guards the paths of justice and preserves the way of His saints. Happy is the man who finds wisdom and happy is the man who understands.

We are blessed for understanding God's plan for the world. The Old Testament reveals that prophets Zephaniah and Joel both prophesized that the Lord would return. The "Great Day of the Lord" is at hand and the "Great Day of the Lord" is coming.

Zephaniah 1:2-3

"I will utterly consume everything
From the face of the land," Says the Lord;
I will consume man and beast;
I will consume the birds of the heaven,
The fish of the sea,
And the stumbling blocks along with the wicked,
I will cut off man from the face of the land,"

Zephaniah 1:7

"Be silent in the presence of the Lord God;
For the day of the Lord is at hand.

In **Joel 2:1-2** it says:

"Blow the trumpet in Zion,
And sound an alarm in My Holy mountain!
Let all the inhabitants of the land tremble;
For the Day of the Lord is coming,

For it is at hand;
A day of darkness and gloominess,
A day of clouds and thick darkness,"

Joel 2:9-11 goes on to say:
"They run to and fro in the city; they run on the wall;
They climb into the houses; they enter at the windows
like a thief.
The earth quakes before them; the heavens tremble;
The sun and moon grow dark and the stars diminish
their brightness.
The Lord gives voice before His army, for His camp is
very great;
For strong is the One who executes His word.
For the day of the Lord is great and very terrible;
Who can endure it?"

The last sentence "who can endure it?" Why would anyone want to challenge themselves to endure times like these when we have another option? The Lord wants us to turn to Him with all our hearts, with fasting, with weeping, with mourning and with repentance.   In **Matthew 4:17** Jesus began to preach and says *"Repent, for the kingdom of heaven is at hand."* We must keep our hearts, minds and souls directed toward Jesus.

We free ourselves from bondage by repenting of our sins. Each and every one of us *sin* every day by our thoughts, our behaviors, and how we treat others. A "sin" is a "sin" no matter how big or how small. Using the Lord's name in vain by swearing is just as sinful as stealing, killing, or dishonoring your parents, but each act of defiance by law requires different discipline. For example, if someone kills another person, the law will require them to serve time in prison for their crime. If you swear using the Lord's name in vain, it is still a sin, but not one that the law requires prison time. Each day we need to repent before God and ask Him to forgive us for our sins. He will forgive us if we are genuinely remorseful and make the effort to change. Keeping our eyes on Jesus will save our souls for eternity.

How do we know the Lord or the Son of Man is coming back to earth? His second coming is certain even though it has been nearly 2,000 years since the birth of Jesus. In the section, "The Signs of the Times and the End of the Age" in **Matthew 24:30-31**, Jesus says to His disciples:

"*Then the sign of the Son of Man will appear in heaven, and then all the tribes of the earth will mourn, and they will see the Son of Man coming on the clouds of heaven with power and great glory. And He will send His angels with a great sound of a trumpet, and they will gather together His elect from the four winds, from one end of heaven to the other.*"

Jesus goes on to say in **Matthew 24:36-44**, "*But of that day and hour no one knows, not even the angels of heaven, but My Father only. But as the days of Noah were, so also will the coming of the Son of Man be. For as in the days before the flood, they were eating and drinking, marrying and giving in marriage, until the day that Noah entered the ark, and did not know until the flood came and took them all away, so also will the coming of the Son of Man be. Then two men will be in the field: one will be taken and the other left. Two women will be grinding at the mill: one will be taken and the other left. Watch therefore, for you do not know what hour your Lord is coming. But know this that if the master of the house had known what hour the thief would come, he would have watched and not allowed* *his house to be broken into. Therefore, you also be ready, for the Son of Man is coming at an hour you do not expect."*

As we read just a few of the Scriptures that describe His second coming, the message is very strong and well-defined; The Son of Man will return. As an author, I feel incapable of adding any other words of my own to this section; for scripture says it in a way that leaves me in "awe." I am speechless when unbelievers debate the second coming when the words "He is Coming" are listed 318 times in the New Testament.

"When you see Jerusalem being surrounded by armies, you will know that its desolation is near; for this is the time of punishment in fulfillment of all that has been written. There will be signs in the sun, moon, and stars. On the earth, nations will be in anguish and perplexity at the roaring and tossing of the sea. Men will faint from terror, apprehensive of what is coming on the world, for the heavenly bodies will be shaken. At that time, they will see the Son of Man, coming in a cloud with power and great glory. When these things begin to take place, stand up and lift up your heads, because your redemption is drawing near." **(Luke 21:20, 25)**

In conclusion, **Revelation 22:20** states *"Surely, I am coming quickly." His followers say "Amen, Even so, come, Lord Jesus!"*

The best is yet to come...it is the hope and excitement of the Second Coming of Christ that gives me peace every day of my life. Jesus is returning to be our King of kings, Lord of lords on earth. If you are a believer in our Lord Jesus Christ, there is something very magnificent we have to look forward to: The 1000 Years of reigning peacefully with Christ and then the New Heaven and Earth. Let's take a look at the beautiful side of Christ's return.

CHAPTER 11

THE NEW HEAVEN & EARTH

It may be hard to realistically picture in our minds right now what the new Heaven and Earth will someday look and feel like, but **Revelation 21-22** gives us a unique depiction of what is to come. The first heaven and earth has passed away after the Great White Throne Judgment.

The Great White Throne Judgment is described by Apostle John in **Revelation 20:11-15 as the following:**

"Then I saw a great white throne and Him who sat on it, from whose face the earth and the heaven fled away. And there was found no place for them. And I saw the dead, small and great, standing before God and the books were opened. And another book was opened, which is the Book of Life. And the dead were judged according to their works, by the things which were written in the books. The sea gave up the dead who were in it, and Death and Hades delivered up the dead who were in them. And they were judged, each one according to his works. Then Death and Hades were

cast into the lake of fire. This is the second death. Anyone not found written in the Book of Life was cast into the lake of fire."

Here we are at this pivotal time when the unbelievers face God on judgment day. God opens the seals of judgment. There is no turning back for their fate is sealed. The people whose names are not written in the Book of Life are cast into the lake of fire and brimstone to be tormented day and night forever and ever. Unbelievers who have been dead since Adam & Eve are now sentenced to an eternity of torture. They join Satan, (the devil), the Antichrist, and the false prophet, all whom God had devoured and thrown into the lake of fire. The judgment of the "unholy" trinity has been complete and all the demons, fallen angels and unbelievers are eternally separated from God.

NEW HEAVEN AND A NEW EARTH

Apostle John writes, "Now I saw a new heaven and a new earth, for the first heaven and the first earth had passed away. Also, there was no more sea. Then I saw the holy city, New Jerusalem, coming down out of heaven from God, prepared as a bride adorned for her husband. And I heard a loud voice from heaven saying, 'Behold, the tabernacle of God is with men, and He will dwell with them, and they shall be His people. God Himself will be with them and be their God." *(Revelation 21:1-3)*

We now have a completely new heaven and earth and the old has passed away. God does away with the earth as we know it today. He also writes there are no more seas. Two-thirds of today's earth is covered with water and the remaining one-third is covered with large areas of mountains and deserts; therefore, only a small area of the earth is livable. In that small area, we have a current population of 7.2 billion people. God is going to dwell with everyone on this earth. This will be better than anything this world has ever known. We shall be His people and He will be present with us as we worship and give Him the glory. *"He will wipe away every tear from their eyes. There will be no more death or mourning or sorrows or crying or pain, for the old order of things are passed away." He (Jesus) who was seated at the throne said "I am making everything new!"*

(Revelation 21:4-5)

What a beautiful feeling to know we will never know pain again. We will not worry about death or mourn any losses for the old way of living on earth has passed. Tears that Jesus will wipe away are not from present pain, shame or guilt, but tears caused by the death, persecution and other hardships that His people suffered on the old earth. I can imagine many pure tears of 'joy' by just residing in the presence and the light of our Lord. The new earth will no longer encounter any evil, sin, chaos or death. Jesus is making everything new and well again as we settle into this new existence for "eternity". We simply do not have the mental capacity to grasp the reality of living in a life where God Himself dwells with us, but it sounds absolutely breathtaking. The New Jerusalem will be the eternal ruling place of Christ and a place of peace for those inhabitants of this new earth. Christ will dwell with us. Can you just imagine Christ residing among us with no more suffering or sorrows?

In **Revelation 21:10-12,** Apostle John writes, *"And He carried me away in the spirit to a great and high mountain, and showed me the great city, the holy Jerusalem, descending out of heaven from God, having the*

GLORY OF GOD. Her light was like a most precious stone, like a jasper stone, clear as crystal. Also she had a great and high wall with twelve gates and twelve angels at the gates, and names written on them, which are the names of the twelve tribes of the children of Israel." John continues to describe the New Jerusalem as a city made out of precious stones with the construction of the walls as jasper and the city as pure gold, like clear glass. The foundations were adorned with precious stones and the twelve gates, each one pearl and the streets of the city were pure gold.

There is no temple in it; for the Lord God Almighty and the Lamb are its temple. The city has no need of the sun or the moon to give light, for the "glory of God" illuminates the New Jerusalem. The Lamb is its light. There is no night there and everyone shall walk in the light of Jesus. There shall be no means of anything that enters this land that defiles or causes an abomination or a lie, but only those who are written in the Lamb's Book of Life.

In **Revelation 22:1-4 NIV**, Apostle John is shown a pure river of water of life; clear as crystal, proceeding from the throne of God and of the Lamb. On each side of the river stood the tree of life, bearing 12 crops of fruit, yielding its fruit every month. The leaves of the tree were for the healing of the nations. There will be no more curses, for the throne of God and of the Lamb shall be in it and His servants shall serve Him. Believers will be able to see the Lord face-to-face. The Lord God gives them light and everyone will reign forever and ever.

Jesus said *"It is done. I am the Alpha and the Omega, the Beginning and the End. To him who is thirsty I will give to drink and he who overcomes will inherit all this and I will be his God and He will be my son."* Interestingly, the more vividly aware we are of His impending return, the more we will be motivated in our work for Him in these last days.

In **Revelation 1:5**, we see that history has an end goal; we see that God is working out His ultimate plan for the world. We can see that God really is in control and that Jesus will ultimately be ruler of all the kings of the earth, standing on Mount of Olives.

THE TIME IN NEAR

"Behold, I am coming quickly! Blessed is he who keeps the words of the prophecy of this book."

(Revelation 22:7)

"And behold, I am coming quickly, and My reward is with Me, to give to everyone according to his work. I am the Alpha and Omega, the Beginning and the End, the First and the Last." ***(Revelation 22:12-13)***

There are only a few scriptures in Revelation when Jesus gives us a blessing (Revelation 1:3, 22:7; 22:14).

As you read the Bible on prophecy you are being blessed by our Lord Jesus Christ. In **Revelation 1:3,** "Blessed is he who reads and those who hear the words of this prophecy, and keep those things which are written in it; for the **time is near**." Are you ready to receive our Lord Jesus as your King of kings and Lord of lords?

Blessed are those who do His commandments, that they may have the right to the tree of life and may enter through the gates into the city.
Revelation 22:14

My peace I give to you; not as the world gives do I give to you. Let not your heart be troubled, neither let it be afraid.
John 14:27

CHAPTER 12

ARE YOU READY?

In this book we have talked about prophetic signs of the end times, the four blood moons, the seven-year cycle of the Shemitah, what is happening in America now and in prophecy, the rapture, the tribulation, and what is to come with the second coming of the Lord and eventually the New Heaven and Earth that awaits all believers.

We have events happening in September 2015 that could change the world as we know it. Christians are keeping their eyes on Jesus as they observe His words, "BE WATCHFUL, ALERT AND ON GUARD" as we stand by and observe what God has in store for our world. The biggest question is "Are You Ready?" If the Lord was to come today, are you ready to receive Him? The time may be closer than we think as we look at events about to happen. Most biblical scholars believe that it is the emergence of all these events at once that cause Christians to believe "something big is about to happen".

In order to follow what God may be mysteriously trying to reveal to us, we need to look at Jewish history and the fall feasts. Many Christians are not familiar with the Jewish Holidays that appear in the autumn season. Remember Jesus was Jewish and these Holy Days are His, so we should have an understanding of what these days mean. (Leviticus 23:1-44) Christians have been talking about several upcoming events that all accumulate in the month of September 2015. I will repeat that this is not the "end of the world", but a time when the world as we know it "ends".

1) **September 13, 2015** is the same date as Hebrew calendar **29 Elul**. This day is the last day of the seven-year cycle of the Sabbath or a "Shemitah". This means "wiping away or the releasing of debt". This date of 29 Elul was also the date of two other major financial downfalls of the stock market. One was after the attack on 9/11 in New York when the stock market reopened on September 17th to a stunning drop of 7% of the market. The second time was seven years later, on the exact date of 29 Elul, when the 2008 stock market fell a record-breaking 777.7 points or 7% of the market on September 29, 2008. This was followed by a global financial crisis, banks closing, foreclosures and job loss throughout the nation. Remember, the number "7" is the Lord's perfect or complete number.

If history repeats itself, the Lord may reveal His harbinger or warning to us once again. In 2015, the 29 Elul falls on September 13th, when Wall Street is closed. Of course, we won't see a drop in stocks on that day, but as Jonathan Cahn points out in his new book, *The Mystery of the Shemitah*, "sometimes stock markets crash a few days before the end, up to two weeks after the end of a Shemitah or Sabbath cycle." The Friday before Sunday the 13th, is

9/11; a date etched into every American's memory as our nation experienced one of the most terrifying attacks on the World Trade Centers, destroying New York's two tallest buildings and unfortunately taking 2,996 American lives, plus misplacing thousands of others. This attack also struck the Pentagon in Washington DC and took down Flight 93 over Pennsylvania. Per Wikipedia, "As of August 2013, another 1,140 people who worked or lived in Lower Manhattan at the time of the attack have been exposed to toxins and diagnosed with cancer. Over 1,400 rescue workers who responded to the scene that day have since died."

The questions remains: What will happen during the end of this seven- year cycle of wiping away or releasing debt?

2) **September 13, 2015** is also the evening beginning with the Hebrew "Feast of Trumpets". The month of Elul, the 29 days, is a period of a call to repentance each day. It is about returning in faith and repentance to our Lord. Each morning during the 29 days of Elul, the trumpet (shofar) or ram's horn is blown to repent and return to God.

"Listen, I tell you a mystery: We will not all sleep, but we will all be changed—in a flash, in the twinkling of an eye, at the last trumpet. For the trumpet will sound, the dead will be raised imperishable, and we will be changed. For the perishable must clothe itself with the imperishable and the mortal with immortality. **(1 Corinthians 15:51-53)**

Some Christians believe this to be the possible day of the rapture, but it is only **speculation** since God is clear in the Word that no one knows the day or the hour Jesus will return for His Church.

3) **September 14, 2015** – This is the first day of the Jewish Holiday "Rosh Hashanah" or "Feast of Trumpets", which lasts 10 days and ends on Yom Kippur, September 23rd. These are known as the High Holy Days and as the Days of Awe. The "Feast of Trumpets" begins on the 7th Hebrew month, 1 Tishri, and introduces the autumn festivals which represent the present age of man and the beginning of an incredible time during which God will play a more direct part in world events. This Holy Day represents a dramatic turning point in world history. The people should be ready and waiting for the awakening blast of the shofar of Rosh Hashanah. (**Numbers 29:1**) *"For you it is a day of blowing the trumpets."* The Feast of Trumpets could be the return of Jesus Christ for His church at the last trump, just before God pours His wrath and judgment out on a sinful and Christ rejecting world. Repent before this date to avoid any judgment during the Days of Awe.

God has always had a heart to warn people before He proclaims judgment. God warned the people before the great flood of Noah's Ark when the earth was flooded and ruined. He does not want anyone to receive the wrath of His judgment. (**Ezekiel 18:21-23, 30-32; Zephaniah 2:1-3**).

4) **September 23, 2015** - "Day of Atonement" begins at sundown on September 22nd and ends at sundown on September 23rd. The final (70th) Jubilee will end on the Day of Atonement in 2015. This day is also referred to as Yom Kippur. This can all be confusing, but stay with me. A Jubilee consists of 50 years and the last year is at the end of seven cycles of Shemitah (sabbatical years) and according to **Leviticus 25:8-13**, slaves and prisoners would be freed, debts would be forgiven and the mercies of God would be

particularly manifested. The Bible describes a period of time most people have never heard of - the Jubilee year. It occurs after seven sets of seven yearly intervals (49 total) are finished. This proclamation of a fiftieth "liberty" year occurs on one of God's annual feast days known as the Day of Atonement. Because God owns everything, he set up a special, regularly occurring time period where His will is that a man's possessions are returned to him.

There will have been 40 complete Jubilee cycles since Christ's death. This is very interesting because the number 40 is a significant number to God and represents "trials, probation, and testing". The 40 Jubilees since Christ's death brings us to the end of provisional time. Jesus was tempted by Satan many times during the 40 days and nights he fasted before His ministry began. He also appeared to His disciples and others for 40 days after His resurrection. Moses spent 40 years in the desert as a shepherd and the children of Israel were punished by wandering the wilderness for 40 years. **(Matthew 24:1-2, Mark 13:1-2).**

David reigned as king on earth for 40-1/2 years.

"And they anointed David king over Israel. David was thirty years old when he began to reign, and he reigned forty years. In Hebron he reigned over Judah seven years and six months, and in Jerusalem he reigned thirty-three years over all Israel and Judah." **(2 Samuel 5:3-5)**

When Jesus ascended into heaven 31 AD and reigns 40-1/2 Jubilee cycles, it takes us to 2015 AD. If David reigned as King on earth for 40-1/2 Jubilee cycles, could it be possible that Jesus will reign as King in Heaven for 40-1/2

Jubilee cycles and then return for His church? This is something to contemplate for 2015.

The 40 Jubilees after Christ's death bring us to the end of probationary time. Forty years after the crucifixion in 70 A.D., the Roman Empire destroyed Jerusalem and burned its beloved temple to the ground. If the time is near, ask yourself these questions: Do I know the Lord? Do I consider the Lord, Jesus Christ to be my one and only savior? Have I repented of all my sins? Time is of the essence...get right with God and put Jesus first in your heart!

4) September 28, 2015 – This is the last day of the last red blood moon that we talked about in Chapter 3. This rare event of a full lunar eclipse and a super moon will fully be on display in Jerusalem and, ironically, appear on the first day of the Jewish Holy Day, "Feast of Tabernacles" or "Sukkot". This festival is the beginning of eight (8) days of celebration from September 28th – October 4, 2015 with October 5, 2015 being the eighth day.

"Lord, will You at this time restore the kingdom to Israel?"   **(Acts 1:6)**

The Feast of Tabernacles represents a coming time of unprecedented harmony and peace, and from a biblical perspective it will be a time when all nations learn of the great things that will happen when people follow the ways of the God.

This festival looks back at the 40-year period when the Israelites lived in the wilderness. During that time the Hebrew people were isolated from the rest of the world, but their needs were taken care of by God. It is a time of dwelling in "booths" or little huts that were temporary dwellings. Today, we could do this in a tent and it would be considered a booth. Would a RV trailer count for being a booth? It might be if it is considered a temporary dwelling; even though it seems like a very extravagant booth. The Feast of Tabernacles is our yearly wilderness experience where we commune with God. It is our opportunity to *"go up to the mountain of the Lord, to the house of the God of Jacob...so that He can teach us His ways and we shall walk in His paths.* **(Isaiah 2:3)**

5) September 15-28, 2015 – The 70th Annual Session of the United Nations General Assembly will open on September 15, 2015. Pope Francis will visit the UN on September 25th and address the world leaders on global climate and how it affects our environment. It is also reported that France plans to introduce a resolution which gives formal recognition to a Palestinian state. This draft would define Israel's pre-1967 borders as a reference point for talks, but also designate Jerusalem as the capital of both Israel and a Palestinian state and call for a fair solution for Palestinian refugees. The United States has blocked this in past sessions, but there are concerns President Obama may have different ideas this time. If this resolution passes, it would be signed on September 28, 2015, our last blood moon. Would this be the start of another big conflict in Israel? It is difficult to imagine Israel and the Palestinians sharing the capital of Jerusalem in a peaceful manner.

DO YOU BELIEVE IN GOD?

I have often wondered why people choose not to believe in a God who created our earth and our heaven. A person can look out at nature, see the blue sky, watch an animal play, watch a baby being born, and be with someone while they are dying, and see the Lord at work. His hands are everywhere. How did our earth come to be in perfect alignment with the sun, moon, and stars and rotate on an axial with perfect rhythm so all four seasons of spring, summer, fall and winter revolve throughout the year? How could our earth be situated in this gigantic universe at the perfect gravitational pull so that we can walk or run anywhere and we don't float off into space? It certainly wasn't man who came up with this idea! God made each of us in the "image of God". In **Genesis 5:1** it states, *"In the day that God created man, He made him in the likeness of God".*

If you feel scared about the information you have just read, it may be a blessing in disguise! It may be a CALL to come closer to the Lord, be in His Word, and bring Him into your Heart where worry, concern and fear disappear! Have you ever worried about the results of a medical procedure? Have you had the anxious week of waiting for the news? Once you find out what it is, even if it isn't the best news, you relax, knowing you now know "what" it is, and then you proceed on to getting the treatment you need. Studying prophecy is much the same way, once you learn about it and all its signs and signals; you can begin to make the changes. Once you feel you are closer to GOD, you will no longer feel the fear! You will actually get very excited about the end and being with our Lord!

"But you, brethren, are not in darkness, so that this Day should overtake you as a thief. You are all sons of light and sons of the day. We are not of the night, nor of darkness. Therefore let us not sleep, as others do, but let us watch and be sober. For God did not appoint us to wrath, but to obtain salvation through our Lord Jesus Christ."
(1 Thessalonians 5:4-6; 9)

Christ gives us firm warnings about the dangers of hell **(Matthew 5:22-30; 10:28)** In many churches, smiling

154

ministers can preach and say glowing words about heaven, but seemingly ignore the scriptures on hell. It seems they don't want to offend the unbelieving and unrepentant. Many Christian authors publish books on having a relationship with God, but fail to disclose what will happen if souls do not belong to Christ. Who would want to live forever in hell in a lake of brimstone and fire forever and forever in a life of torment with no end in sight?

DO YOU WANT TO BE RAPTURED?

I think all of us believers want to be raptured and be in the Heavens with our Lord. Surprisingly, there are people who call themselves Christians, yet rarely open their bibles to read the Word and worship our Lord. There are people who are very bible smart and very intellectual to answer most questions, yet do not have Jesus in their **hearts**. What does it mean to have Jesus in your heart?

One of the best examples is to think about a loved one, someone you really love. You want to do nice things for them; help them with a project; place a phone call to them to just say, "I love you"; buy them flowers; send them a card; randomly touch them on the arm to say, "I care"; you want them to be comfortable and so and so on. Loving God and Jesus is the same way. If you love Jesus in your heart, you want to reach out and do something special for Him. It may be singing His songs, reading His words in the Bible, sharing your beliefs with a friend, helping out a homeless person, or babysitting for a single mom. For me personally, it was writing this book for God. We want to show Him through our works that we love Him and will follow what He wants us to do. This is loving Jesus with our hearts just like you would love a husband, wife or child. Look at the list below and see how you can ask Jesus into your heart:

1) Make sure that you have received Jesus Christ into your life as your PERSONAL Lord and Savior.

Most people want to be baptized as a symbol of demonstrating that their lives have been converted to a "born again" faith in Jesus. To the new converts and believers in **Acts 2:41** and **Acts 8:13, 16,** it was inconceivable that one would come to faith in Jesus Christ and not be baptized.

2) Repent, repent, and repent! Ask the Lord for forgiveness of your sins and then turn completely away from the sin(s) and turn completely towards Jesus. All sin separates us from God, even as a Christian.

3) Stay in the Word on a daily basis and set aside quiet time to be with our Lord. This simple act of taking 10-30 minutes and being STILL with Him as you read scripture can add measurable peacefulness to each day.

4) Listen to His Whispers. In our stillness or quiet times with the Lord, we may hear whispers or a repeated message in our minds to do something for the Lord. With discernment, follow what the Lord asks you to do for He works through all people who believe in Him. (Caution: If you hear a message to do something evil, against the law, or against the moral law of the 10 Commandments, this is not the Lord speaking; it is the voice of Satan.)

5) Listen for God's voice and then STAY OPEN TO THE LEADING OF THE HOLY SPIRIT. Act upon that which the Lord is calling you to do. *"He who has an ear, let him hear"*. We need to listen to what God wants us to do. If you are not certain it is God speaking to you, then wait until the message is clearer or repeated.

6) Draw closer to God by praying, reading His Word, attending a Bible-based church as often as possible, and surround yourself with a Christian atmosphere (Christian friends, books, music, radio, TV, etc.) The encouragement and inspiration of other Christians directs us away from sin and encourages us to lead a more holy life.

7) Examine your own heart for any signs of backsliding, being of the world, not being watchful, or being lukewarm. In **Revelation 3:15-16,** it states, "*I know your works, that you are neither cold or hot. I could wish you were cold or hot. So then, because you are lukewarm, I will vomit you out of My mouth.*" Not a pleasant sight, but it is clear God wants us to be "passionate" about Him.

8) Getting our life and our loved ones' spiritual house in order with Jesus is essential. **John 14:6**, "*I am the way, the truth, and the life, no one comes to the Father but by me.*"

9) Study end-time Biblical prophecy until you become completely convinced that His Coming is, indeed, AT THE DOOR. This will help keep you from temptation and sin and help you to live a peaceful life.

"Blessed is he who reads and those who hear the words of this prophecy and keep those things which are written in it; for the time is near."
(Revelation 1:3)
10) Put our efforts into reaching others' **souls** to seek Jesus by witnessing to them. This may take the form of talking or evangelizing, sending a bible or book to someone needing encouragement, sending a Christian card, helping others with food and shelter, teaching to adults or children, making

that important phone call to say you are thinking about someone, or praying for them. Being a witness for the Lord takes on many different forms and choosing a method that is on your heart is more important than trying to do them all.

11) **"PRAY, PRAY, PRAY"** (Psalms 55:17) **"Pray without ceasing"** (1 Thessalonians 5:16) Set aside a designated time and place for prayer each day. Be very still, concentrate on your prayers and be quiet with the Lord. As you get into a routine it will become easier. Some people love the early morning hours; others love the evening hours when the house is quiet. Whatever time is right for you to pray, it is right for God. He loves hearing your prayers and your praise.

What if I don't know how to pray? God loves ordinary, simple words that come straight from your heart. He already knows your heart, so let the words flow, no matter how uncomfortable you may feel. The Lord loves the humble, the meek, and the poor, so any words you pray, He will receive them. Ask for his guidance, ask for what you need, ask for help, be vulnerable and then thank him for his love. Always give Him the glory and the praise for He is the giver of life. Some prayers are answered right away and some are not answered for an obvious reason or a reason unknown to you. Perhaps, He does not want you to go that direction. As you learn to "listen" in for the answers to prayers, you will learn to decipher how he wants you to proceed in life. It truly is a beautiful thing. The Lord hears every thought in your mind, so be careful what you think.

Jesus is on your side. He wants the very best for you. You're a royal priesthood belonging to God **(1 Peter 2:9)**.

And despite what the world is telling you about whether to believe, what to believe, and how to live your life, put your confidence and complete faith in Jesus Christ today.

Now more than ever Christians need to have a deeper understanding of the Bible so that they have a fuller understanding as to how current events may fit into the larger context of God's plan for the last days.

Let's take a look at how we can fully live a life that shows Jesus that we BELONG to Him.

"Whoever desires to come after Me, let him
deny himself, and take up his cross
and follow Me."
Mark 8:34

CHAPTER 13

LIVE LIKE YOU "BELONG" TO GOD

How do we know for certain that we are living today like we "belong" to God? If you were to ask 4 different people who identify themselves as Christians, you would get 4 different answers. According to Bible Study Planet.com, as we research the New Testament, we find at least four different types of Christians:

THE DEAD CHRISTIAN

Jesus says in the letter to the church in Sardis:

"I know your works, that you have a name that you are alive, but you are dead." **(Revelation 3:1)**

The Dead Christian is a person who calls himself a Christian in name only. This type of Christian may go to church, either occasionally or regularly, and may claim to follow Christ, but hasn't truly come to Jesus for honest repentance or forgiveness.

Jesus spoke to the Dead Christian in **Revelation 3:2-3** when he goes on to say, "*Be watchful, and strengthen the things which remain, that are ready to die, for I have not found your works perfect before God. Remember therefore how you have received and heard, hold fast and repent.*" What 'works' of God did He find to be incomplete? We find the answers in **John 6:24**, "*he who hears My word and believes in Him who sent Me, has everlasting life, and shall not come into judgment, but pass from death into life.*" A Dead Christian may go to church, sit in the pews, listen to the sermon, but never actually receive Jesus into his/her heart by repenting and asking for forgiveness.

1 John 5:11-13 vividly states as, "*And this is the testimony: that God has given us eternal life, and this life is in His Son. He who has the Son has 'life'; he who does not have the Son of God does not have life. These things I have written to you who believe in the name of the Son of God….*"

Tom identifies himself as a Christian because he attends church with his wife, Martha, on a regular basis. He watches the time on the clock as the sermon is preached, anxiously waiting for the dismissal, so he can run to the Family Center to get coffee and doughnuts. He refuses to carry his Bible as it does not look very manly. At home, he prefers reading a good thriller novel versus sitting and studying scripture. Tom is a Dead Christian.

THE BOUND CHRISTIAN

The Bound Christian is one who is alive in Christ, but is bound by sin and this hinders his/her relationship with the Lord. In **Galatians 5:22-24**, we can summarize by saying, *"the works of the flesh are evident….just as I also told you in time past, that those who practice such things will not inherit the kingdom of God."*

"For the flesh lusts against the Spirit and the Spirit against the flesh; and these are contrary to one another, so that you do not do the things that you wish."

Galatians 5:17

Fred loves the Lord and has been a Christian for 20 years. He attends a bible study faithfully every Wednesday night at his friend's house and helps out at church whenever needed. He still battles with alcoholism and manages to hide it from his church friends. On weekends he goes out to the local bar and drinks until he is very drunk and his bar friends have to drive him home. He gets angry at his family for asking him to change and get help for his addiction. Fred is a Bound Christian.

THE LONER CHRISTIAN

The Loner Christian is alive and enjoys his/her time learning and worshiping God. His/her life is full of blessings, but the Loner Christian keeps his blessings to himself. They do want to reach out and share their abundance with others.

Hebrew 10:23-24 states, *"Let us hold fast the confession of our hope without wavering, for He who promised is faithful. And let us consider one another in order to stir up love and good works."*

Jesus said in **John 10:10**, *"that we may have life and have it abundantly."* And in that abundance, He asked us to give and bless others. We all are blessed with many gifts (encouragement, teaching, prayer, compassion, helping, etc) and we have received those gifts by the grace of our Lord. Sharing those gifts with others inspires them to draw closer to the Lord thus receiving the added benefit of feeling blessed. The Loner Christian keeps their gifts for serving themselves.

Lillian is a faithful follower of Jesus Christ. She attends church every single Sunday and is proud of her spotless attendance. She reads her bible daily and attends the Women's Bible Study religiously every Thursday. She chooses not to interact with others. When asked to help out at any of the church potlucks or the Sunday school she always declines. Deep down she doesn't enjoy any of the social events and doesn't care to interact with the people of the church. She leaves the "helping" to other people. Lillian is a Loner Christian.

THE COMPLETE CHRISTIAN

The Complete Christian has a strong relationship with God, feels alive in Christ, and is a blessing to others. The Complete Christian attends church to worship the Lord; they read their Bible daily to stay connected to God; they attend or hold bible studies; they are not afraid to stand up for God; they are a great witness for the Lord; they help others as needed and most importantly, they glorify our Father in everything they do.

Ephesians 2:10 states, *"For we are His workmanship, created in Christ Jesus for good works, which God prepared beforehand that we should walk in them."*

Matthew 5:16 says, *"Let your light so shine before men, that they may see your good works and glorify your Father in heaven."*

The Complete Christians live their lives in a way that when people see them, they see Jesus and God glorified. Their love for God shines forth for everyone to see and admire. They are humble and speak about their Lord in a loving way.

Jennifer is studying Christian counseling at her local university. She has attended church most of her life and is a leader for her church's youth group. She is liked and loved by most people she meets because of her joyful love for God. She stays connected to God by listening to worship music, reads her bible daily in the morning before she leaves the house. She prays for others, and spends most of her time interacting with other Christians. She also is a great witness for Jesus as she shares her faith. Once a year, she attends a silent retreat to get closer to God and renew her heart. Jennifer is a Complete Christian.

Todd is also a Complete Christian. During his twenties he was addicted to heroin and drank beer every night. He lost his wife of four years and custody of his young son because of his continual drug/alcohol problems. At the age of 32, he finally hit rock bottom considering suicide as a way out of his misery. A volunteer for suicide prevention talked Todd into going to a rehab center for drug & alcohol. During his time there a counselor asked him to reach out for Christ and pray for healing. After two years of sobriety and hard work, he found the help he needed to live a more productive life. He started going to church, reading his bible and changed his friends to other Christian believers. God answered his prayers by giving him visitations with his young son. Todd invited Jesus to reside in his heart and with continued prayer and learning, his life changed for the better. Todd is a Complete Christian.

FINAL INSTRUCTIONS FOR LIVING TO PLEASE GOD

Yes, God did leave final instructions for how to live to please Him. He is such a loving Father! He doesn't leave us guessing on how to live; he actually left us final instructions and commandments. I love it! **1 Thessalonians 4-5** (NIV) gives us a list by the authority of our Lord Jesus:

- Live a holy life! Follow the 10 Commandments! **(Exodus 20)**
- Love one another. Love all your brothers and sisters not only in Christ, but in the world. Live in peace with one another.
- Make it your ambition to lead a quiet life, to mind your own business and to work with your hands, so your

daily life may win the respect of outsiders and so that you will not be dependent on others.

- Respect those who work hard among you and who are leaders over you.
- Warn those who are idle with their hands; encourage the timid and help the weak.
- Be patient with everyone; always try to be kind to each other.
- Make sure nobody pays back wrong for wrong.
- Be joyful, pray continually without ceasing, and give thanks in ALL circumstances for this is God's will for you in Christ Jesus.
- Do not put out the Spirit's fire.
- Do not treat prophecies with contempt. You are blessed by reading prophecy.
- Test everything. Hold on to the good.
- Avoid every kind of evil.

OTHER INSTRUCTIONS and TEN COMMANDMENTS:

- Receive Jesus Christ into your life as your personal Lord and Savior. This is the most important aspect of having a personal relationship with Jesus. Receive Him into your heart and ask Him to reside there and guide you with your life. You will be astonished with the surprises He leaves with you.
- Listen to His voice and stay open to the leading of the Holy Spirit. Sometimes we don't recognize the voice as the Holy Spirit. If we continue to listen the voice will appear again. Once you hear it a couple of times, you are being nudged to follow.
- Examine your own heart for being of the world or lukewarm in your love for Jesus.

- Repent, ask for forgiveness! Be sincere and apologize! Sin separates you from God, even as a Christian.
- Confess your sins; He is faithful to cleanse our sins.
- Study end-time Bible prophecy until you are convinced the Lord is indeed coming back and you have no doubt!
- Stay in the Word; study the Books of the Bible.
- Keep your eyes on Jesus even through troubling times.
- Ten Commandments in a short version. The longer version of Exodus 20 is listed in *Notes and References* in the back of this book.

TEN COMMANDMENTS

1. You shall have no other gods before Me.
2. You shall not make idols.
3. You shall not take the name of the LORD your GOD in vain.
4. Remember the Sabbath day, to keep it holy.
5. You shall honor your mother and your father.
6. You shall not murder.
7. You shall not commit adultery.
8. You shall not steal.
9. You shall not bear false witness against your neighbor.
10. You shall not covet. (want or desire)

PUT ON THE ARMOR OF GOD

To truly live like we "belong" to God, we need to be ready to stand up for Him. Christians and Jews are currently being persecuted, attacked and killed all over different parts of the world.

Ephesians 6:11 NIV says, *"We have God's armor on as we go to battle. God promises us that He will give us strength." Verse 17..."therefore put on the full armor of God, so that when the day of evil comes, you may be able to stand your ground."*

Today in our world we hear of Christians being killed among different countries of the Middle East. In 2014, over 120,000 Christians were killed and few people spoke out against it! On the shores of Libya, we hear of 21 Egyptian Christians, each clad in an orange jumpsuit, being beheaded; we realize that they have on "the full armor of God", as they sing songs to Jesus. True martyrs for Jesus Christ are not just in Bible stories of ancient times; they exist today, all over the world. These 21 Christian men are heroes of the faith.

On the CNN news in June 2015, nine people were killed in South Carolina attending a bible study in their church. The shooter walked in the door and asked to sit down by the pastor and for an hour participated in the bible study. They welcomed him with open arms and then he opened fire on them. Now, they believe the shooting was more racially motivated than Christian persecution, but it does show us that we are not safe even in our own churches. He later said in an interview "that he almost decided not to shoot them because they were so nice". Instead of being very angry, the church and the community gave back "love" to that young man. They forgave him and prayed for him. No, it does not erase one moment of the hurt, grief, and pain, but it does show in their faith that they "belong" to God. God will take care of the shooter and they can forgive.

Ephesians 6:19 *"Pray also for me that whenever I open my mouth, words may be given me so that I will* *fearlessly make known the mystery of the gospel...pray that I may declare it fearlessly as I should."*

This scripture reminds me of one Monday morning; I was in the living room working quietly on my laptop, preparing for a class on prophecy. I was putting the final touches on twenty pages of teaching notes. As I hit "save", my laptop opened a window and said, "if you save this file, it may be harmful to your computer; if you trust the contents of this document, you may open it." I laughed thinking "well this is my document and I know what is in it, so I opened the document and then tried to "save" it again under a different name. Again, it would not allow me to save my document. I started to panic because I didn't want to lose all my notes and have to redo them. I decided to trick the computer and "print" them before I lost them forever. I clicked on "print" and waited for the sound of my wireless printer to print in the other room. There was not a sound! I looked down at my computer and it said "printer attempt failed, you cannot print this document unless you save it." I felt such panic rise up inside me, fear of losing everything I had worked on for weeks, and even though I was trying to be calm, I had thoughts that someone in the hacking world was trying to prevent me from teaching this message. The hackers were trying to frustrate me into giving up! Without thinking, I felt the need to grab my Bible, stand up in the middle of the room, and proclaim in a loud voice, "SATAN LEAVE THIS ROOM, SATAN LEAVE THIS ROOM, I am a Believer in JESUS CHRIST and I believe He will come again, LEAVE this ROOM!!!!!" At that very moment, I heard my printer start up in the other room. I was dumb-founded and in complete shock. I couldn't believe my ears; my document was printing! God was right there, in my living room, helping me through this dilemma. He was "PRINTING" my document. I felt so humbled that I fell to my knees and thanked Him with my head down in prayer! I shook with excitement, yet disbelief, as I realized that God responded in such a quick way. He does want me to get this information out. After that incident, I did not have any more problems saving or printing documents.

God wants us to STAND boldly for him. When he asks us to do something for him, he wants us to completely trust in Him. He will work out the details if we KEEP OUR EYES ON JESUS!

Hebrew 11:6 (NIV) *"Without faith it is impossible to please Him."* We cannot worry and trust Him at the same time. Just keep your eyes on Jesus, keeping your blinders on to any side distractions that keep you from focusing on Jesus at all times. Your relationship will deepen with Jesus as you worship, praise, and be obedient to his Word.

1 Thessalonians 2:13 (NIV) *"For this reason we also thank God without ceasing, because when you received the word of God which you heard from us, you welcomed it not as the word of man, but as it is in truth, the word of God, which also, effectively works in you who believe."*

Despite all the evil and destruction you see now in the World, there will be more! We, as true Christians, want to be as close to God as humanly possible. We want to be raptured up to be with our Lord, to be part of His army of angels when He returns the second time. We definitely do not want to be part of the tribulation period.

This is a time in history when millions of us need to stand up for God, His glory, and His righteousness. It is only by the Grace of God that we are worthy to stand up for Him. You were made in the image of God...He wants you!

171

"Bless those who persecute you; bless and do not curse. Rejoice with those who rejoice; mourn with those who mourn. Live in harmony with one another." (**2 Timothy 3:12**) In fact, everyone who wants to live a holy life in Christ Jesus will be persecuted in some form or another.

2 Timothy 1:7 says, *"God has not given us a spirit of fear, but of power and of love and of a sound mind."* I learned a long ago that if I'm living in fear, I'm not living by faith. **1 John 4:18** tells us that perfect love casts out all fear, because fear only brings punishment and torment. Today, if you are prone to be paranoid or fearful of people or circumstances, take Jesus' words to heart; *"Let not your heart be troubled".* (**John 14:27**)

We can all rejoice in the wonderful thought that Jesus will come again; possibly sooner than we can imagine. Am I Ready? A most definite YES! Are you Ready? Only you can answer this question.

What a day it will be when we can **all** say "HALLELIJAH, THE LORD IS COMING."

"If what you heard from the beginning abides in you, you also will abide in the Son and in the Father. And this is the promise that he has promised us---eternal life."
1 John 2:24-25

> **And from Jesus Christ, the faithful witness, the firstborn from the dead, and the ruler over the kings of the earth. To Him who loved us and washed us from our sins in His own blood, and has made us kings and priests to His God and Father, to Him be glory and dominion forever and ever. Amen.**
> **Revelation 1:5-6**

CHAPTER 14

HALLELIJAH, THE LORD IS COMING!

In conclusion, it is an exciting time to know our Lord is indeed returning to be King of kings over all the Earth. Even though we do not know the exact hour or day, the Bible gives us many signs, signals, and prophetic clues that help unlock the mystery. The Rapture of the Church is near and as we come closer to the great trumpet sounds, we must repent and turn to God!

If you consider yourself to be a Christian, take time now to repent, pray, and revive your soul. Spend more quiet time with the Lord. Be bold and ask Him this question, "what can I do for you today?" In your stillness, pray for others and be thankful for all your blessings. Stay in the Word of the Bible and put on the armor of God ready to stand tall to defend Him.

If you would like to invite Jesus into your heart for the very first time, repent of your sins and ask the Lord for forgiveness of your sins. Ask the Lord to be your one and only personal savior. After all, He gave His life for us; He gave His body and His blood so we are covered for our sins. He can fill the emptiness with His love and fellowship for you.

Revelation 3:20 says, *"Behold, I stand at the door and knock; if any one hears my voice and opens the door, I will come in to him and eat with him, and he with me."* At this point, you have invited Jesus to come into your heart. This is just the beginning of a life filled with peacefulness as you begin the journey to love our God. Many people choose to be baptized, purchase their own Holy Bible and begin to attend a local bible-based church. Find a pastor, minister or Christian friend and begin your heart-warming program of worshiping Jesus today. You will immediately feel the difference in your life as His love enters your heart. **John 14:23** says, *"If a man loves me, he will keep my word, and my Father will love him, and we will come to him and make our home with him."*

Proverbs 3:5-6 *"Trust in the Lord with all your heart, and lean not on your own understanding; In all your ways acknowledge Him, and He shall direct your paths."*

2 Chronicles 7:14 (The Message) *"I'll be there ready for you: I'll listen from heaven, forgive their sins, and restore their land to health."*

Today, we are witnessing a global pattern of prophetic signs that indicate we are in the end of times. No, this does not mean the end of the world, but the end of the age as we know it. Our world will change and never return to what we know today. The things that are coming upon America and the rest of the world are coming because mankind has consistently turned a deaf ear away from God. Amazingly, if you are a true believer, you have no fear for God has it totally within His control. It is a very exciting time. If you feel fear about what is happening in our world, then it is a call from Jesus to come closer to Him. He has it all under control.

Therefore, if you don't know God or you are not as close to God as you would like to be; please turn to Him right now for time is running out. To reject God's Savior is to reject God's salvation. To accept both is to honor Him as Lord and God.

God asked us to be Watchful, Be Alert, and Be On Guard! Let's keep our eyes on Jesus as we listen and watch the World change right before our eyes. Keep our eyes on what happens in the world during the end of the Shemitah year, the fall festival Holy Days, the last red blood moon, and the week of the Feast of Tabernacles. They all accumulate together in September of 2015. What message or warning does Jesus want to give us?

Watching the decline of morals and values around the World is painful to observe. It also hurts our Lord. After all, He gave His life for us, so we may be forgiven and repent of our sins. So simple, all we have to do is love Jesus with all of our heart, our mind and our soul and we will be saved and spend eternity in the new Heaven and Earth with Him. Jesus is our One and Only Savior. God is God and we are not.

Even with these words, there will be many souls who still want to control their own environment and not be obedient to God. Unfortunately, the road is wide with lots of company around them so it is easier to follow the wider road than the narrow road of obedience and honor to our Lord Jesus Christ.

God gave us free will; that precious opportunity to choose which road you will take. The good news is that if you are a loyal follower of Jesus Christ, your redemption draws near. The bad news is, if you are not, then you will endure what Jesus Himself calls, the worse period of tribulation (Matthew 24:21) the world has ever seen. If you don't want to go through this time, then you simply need to invite Jesus into your heart today.

Our nation should be calling out to the Lord in desperation, begging His forgiveness of our sins. We don't need more **rights,** we need **Jesus Christ**! In Revelation, we see that history has an end goal; we see that God is working out His ultimate plan for the world. We can see that God really is in control and that Jesus will ultimately be King over all the kings of the earth, ruling and reigning from Jerusalem.

Ready or Not the Lord is Coming for His Church soon!

Now when these things begin to happen, look up and lift up your heads, because your redemption draws near.
Luke 21:28

Jesus said, "I am the way, the truth, and the life. No one comes to the Father except through Me."
John 14:6

NOTES & REFERENCES

CHAPTER 1:   AM I READY?

1. Tim LaHaye and Thomas Ice, *Charting the End Times*, Harvest House Publishers, 2001, p. 11

2. *The Holy Bible*, The International Version, Zondervan, Grand Rapids, Michigan, 2003; All scripture quotations used from this source are indicated. Used by permission. All rights reserved.

CHAPTER 2 SIGNS OF THE END OF THE AGE

1. *Strong's Expanded Exhaustive Concordance of the Bible*, 2001 Thomas Nelson Publishers, page 226 Greek Dictionary, 4592.
2. https://www.jewishvirtuallibrary.org/jsource/ Statistics on Jewish Population in Israel: Updated April 2015
3. *www.inquisitr.com/.../asteroid-impact-apocalypse-2015-mass-anxiety-as-conspiracy-theorists-predict-catastrophe/*
4. www.wikipedia.org/wiki/List_of_famines, June 2015
5. http://www.globalresearch.ca/global-famine/8877, June 2015
6. *www.independent.co.uk/.../almost-a-billion-go-hungry-worldwide-8007759.html* – June 2015
7. http://theeconomiccollapseblog.com/archives/there-will-be-pestilences-why-are-so-many-deadly-diseases-breaking-out-all-over-the-globe-right-now October 2014
8. http://www.cdc.gov/vhf/ebola/outbreaks/2014-west-africa/case-counts.html - June 2015
9. http://www.historytoday.com/ole-j-benedictow/black-death-greatest-catastrophe-ever
10. http://www.internationalrelations.com/wars-in-progress/
11. www.livescience.com/46576-more-earthquakes-still-random-process.html
12. http://www.crystalinks.com/earthquakes.html
13. http://www.guardianlv.com/2015/05/earthquake-in-nevada-brings-range-of-reactions/#iTuKir7yMTGhcEUd.99

14. http://earthquake.usgs.gov/earthquakes/
15. http://www.oregonlive.com/pacific-northwest-news/index.ssf/2015/06/9_earthquakes chikungunya/story
16. abcnews.go.com/Health/heck-?id=24619611
17. http://listverse.com/2010/11/02/10-greatest-killers-of-man
18. *www.who.int/gho/hiv/en/*

CHAPTER 3: **FOUR BLOOD MOONS**

1. Mark Biltz, *Blood Moons, Published by WND Books,* 2014, p. ix (foreword by Joseph Farah), p 145,
2. www.theblaze.com/.../are-**blood-moons**-a-biblical-sign-from-god-that-something-earth-shattering-is-about-to-happen Glenn Beck/John Hagee interview
3. http://www.prophecynewswatch.com/2015/May07/
4. bloodmoons.psalm23central.co

CHAPTER 4: AMERICA: LAND OF THE FREE & THE LOST

1. Pew Research Center, dated December 2012.
2. Walid Shoebat, *God's War on Terror*, Top Executive Media, 2010, p.20-21
3. Website: U.S. National Debt, www.usgovernmentdebt.us, April 2015
4. Website: www.nti.org/threats/nuclear/ Nuclear Threat Initiative, April 2015
5. Website: American Psychological Association, www.apa.org

Chapter 5: WARNING AMERICA: THE SHEMITAH

1. Jonathan Cahn, *The Mystery of the Shemitah*, Published by Frontline, 2014, various pages
2. http://www.federalreservehistory.org/Events/DetailView/48 (Black Monday stock market)
3. http://fortune.com/2013/02/03/the-great-bond-massacre-fortune-1994/ Bond Massacre

4. http://www.investopedia.com/financial-edge/0911/how-september-11-affected-the-u.s.-stock-market, 9/11 Attack and Stock Market Crisis

5. http://money.cnn.com/2008/09/29/markets/markets_newyork/ Global Crisis 2008

6. http://thomas-stanton.com/wp-content/uploads/2012/09/The-Failure-of-Fannie-Mae-and-Freddie-Mac.pdf

7. http://www.newrepublic.com/article/119187/mortgage-foreclosures-2015

8. Interview with Billy Graham, Troy Anderson, writer for Reuters, WND, Charisma and many other media outlets. Troy is also President and editor-in-chief of the World Prophecy Network.

CHAPTER 6: DISCOVERING PROPHECY
No References
CHAPTER 7: AMERICA IN PROPHECY

1.   Tim LaHaye & Thomas Ice, *Charting the End Times*, Harvest House Publishers, 2001, p13

2.   Ron Rhodes, *The Popular Dictionary of Bible Prophecy*, Harvest House Publishers, 2010, p. 23

3.   News.max.com website: David Petraeus interview on 6/14/15 about safety of electric and water grids.

4. Grant Jeffrey, *"One Nation, Under Attack: How Big-Government Liberals are Destroying the America You Love,"* Bible prophecy teacher and author of 30 books.

CHAPTER 8:   THE RAPTURE

1. Tim LaHaye, *A Quick Look at the Rapture & the Second Coming*, *Harvest House Publishers, 2013, p.15*

2. Dr. David Jeremiah, *The Jeremiah Study Bible*, Worthy Publishing, 2013, p.1843.

3. Ron Rhodes, *The End Times in Chronological Order, Harvest House Publishers, 2012, p.41*

4. Ron Rhodes, *The Popular Dictionary of Bible Prophecy*, Harvest House Publishers, 2010, p. 139

5) www.worldometer.info. Statistics on Christianity

CHAPTER 9: SEVEN YEARS OF TRIBULATION

1. http://www.foxnews.com/world/2013/06/02/vatican-spokesman-claims-100000-christians-killed-annually
2. http://www.prophecynewswatch.com/2014/October17/173

Chapter 10: THE SECOND COMING OF CHRIST

1. Dr. David Jeremiah, *What in the World is Going On*, Worthy Publishing, 2013.

2. Fern Flaming, Instructor for Women's Ministry, Ranch Chapel, Lecture on Proverbs, April 2015.

Chapter 11: NEW HEAVEN & EARTH
No References
Chapter 12: ARE YOU READY?
1. https://en.wikipedia.org/wiki/Casualties_of_the_September_11 Statistics
2. Jonathan Cain, *The Mystery of the Shemitah*, Frontline Publishers, 2014
3. http://www.fivedoves.com/letters/oct2011/bge1010-1.htm Jewish Holy Days
4. http://www.sooj.org/ Season of Joy website – Feast of Tabernacles
5. http://sd.iisd.org/events/70th-session-of-the-un-general-assembly-unga-70/

CHAPTER 13: LIVE LIKE YOU BELONG TO GOD

1. http://biblestudyplanet.com/four-types-of-christians/
2. http://lifehopeandtruth.com/bible/10-commandments
3. http://www.cbn.com/cbnnews/insideisrael/2014/Oct Christians-Jews-Team-Up-to-Fight Islamic Persecution

4. CNN News, 6/20/2015 "Nine killed in South Carolina church"
5. Ten Commandments, Exodus 20 Short Version & Longer Version

CHAPTER 14: HALLELIJAH, THE LORD IS COMING

1. Eugene Peterson, *The Message*, NavPress Publishing, 2003, 2 Chronicles 7:14, p 712

The 10 Commandments List in Exodus 20:2-17

1. "I am the LORD your God, who brought you out of the land of Egypt, out of the house of bondage. You shall have no other gods before Me."
2. "You shall not make for yourself a carved image—any likeness of anything that is in heaven above, or that is in the earth beneath, or that is in the water under the earth; you shall not bow down to them nor serve them.
3. "You shall not take the name of the LORD your God in vain, for the LORD will not hold him guiltless who takes His name in vain."
4. "Remember the Sabbath day, to keep it holy. Six days you shall labor and do all your work, but the seventh day is the Sabbath of the LORD your God. Therefore the LORD blessed the Sabbath day and hallowed it."
5. "Honor your father and your mother, that your days may be long upon the land which the LORD your God is giving you."
6. "You shall not murder."
7. "You shall not commit adultery."
8. "You shall not steal."
9. "You shall not bear false witness against your neighbor."
10. "You shall not covet your neighbor's house; you shall not covet your neighbor's wife, nor his male servant, nor His female servant, nor his ox, nor his donkey, nor anything that is your neighbor's."

The Lord's Prayer

Our Father, which art in heaven,
Hallowed be thy Name.
Thy Kingdom come.
Thy will be done in earth,
As it is in heaven.
Give us this day our daily bread.
And forgive us our trespasses,
As we forgive them that trespass against us.
And lead us not into temptation,
But deliver us from evil.
For thine is the kingdom,
The power, and the glory,
Forever and ever.
Amen.

(Taken from the Anglican Book of Common Prayer, 1662)

++

For additional copies or more information on prophecy go to our website:

Website: http://readyornotthelordiscoming.com

Email: Susan@readyornotthelordiscoming.com
   Or   susanfree@live.com

Made in the USA
Middletown, DE
23 July 2015